A CAREER
IN
CLINICAL PSYCHOLOGY

A CAREER IN CLINICAL PSYCHOLOGY: FROM TRAINING TO EMPLOYMENT

ROBERT HENLEY WOODY
AND
MALCOLM HIGGINS ROBERTSON

International Universities Press, Inc.
Madison, Connecticut

Library of Congress Cataloging-in-Publication Data

Woody, Robert Henley.
  A career in clinical psychology : from training to employment / by Robert Henley Woody and Malcolm H. Robertson.
    p.   cm.
  Includes bibliographical references and index.
  ISBN 0-8236-0652-X
  1. Clinical psychology—Vocational guidance. I. Robertson, Malcolm H. II. Title.
RC467.95.W663   1996
616.89'023—dc20   96-25086
                                                          CIP

Manufactured in the United States of America

Dedication

We recognize that our careers and this book have been facilitated by the support and love of our families. We dedicate this book to our spouses, Jane Divita Woody and Joan M. Robertson, and to our children, Jennifer, Robert, and Matthew Woody, and Tim, Suzanne, Greg, Chris, and Michelle Robertson.

Contents

Introduction

We were gratified by the positive response to our book *Becoming a Clinical Psychologist* (1988). As we began work on a second edition, we were struck by the profound changes that had occurred within clinical psychology during the quite brief intervening period. We soon realized, and the publisher concurred, that a complete revision was called for. Thus, we began work on a new book, only to discover that the amount of recent research and activities in the field required two books, this one and its companion volume *Theories and Methods for Practice of Clinical Psychology*.

As might be surmised from the dedication, the authors have, in addition to their own academic experiences, shared the quest (and expenses) for university training with their children. Consequently, while both authors meet and talk with undergraduate and graduate students daily, this book was predicated on experience with a young person's efforts to obtain the academic preparation necessary to enter into rewarding professional employment. Also, practitioners with years of experience have reported how important it is to stay aware of the continuum from training to employment. Therefore, this book was tailored to provide information that would help the reader gain the best possible preparation for entering or effective continuation in the field of clinical psychology.

Based on the belief that understanding the present and planning for the future requires understanding of the past, chapter 1, "History and Evolution 1: From the Early Years to 1980," traces the dynamic and remarkable developments that have occurred in clinical psychology from its foundation in the late nineteenth century until 1980. By the 1960s, clinical psychology had progressed to the point where it received profound public policy and governmental support, but the regressive economy and changes in political priorities resulted in employment problems for graduates in the 1970s. With ingenuity, the profession regrouped, engaged in strategic planning, and moved forward with new zest.

Chapter 2, "History and Evolution II: The Mature Years, 1980 to the Mid-1990s," shows that the 1980s found schisms developing between clinical psychology and other psychological specialties. Nonetheless, widespread public policy and governmental recognition was granted to clinical psychology, as it became part of the health care industry and rewards flowed freely to clinicians. Health care reform and managed health care systems, however, introduced new challenges. Consequently, the 1990s led to uncertainty about the future, but (as will be discussed in chapter 8) there is an unprecedented potential for new roles.

Entering the profession and eventually having a successful career requires having proper and, preferably, distinguished qualifications. Chapter 3, "Becoming Trained I: Academic Preparation," describes the accreditation of clinical psychology training programs and the different training models (notably the scientist–practitioner and the practitioner–professional models), and reveals the criteria that training programs use to select applicants for admission.

Since clinical psychology is more than academics per se, chapter 4, "Becoming Trained II: Supervised Clinical

Experiences and Critical Issues," examines practicum, internship, and postdoctoral clinical training. Supervision is explained, and information provided for locating a clinical training opportunity.

Every clinical psychologist should give unabashed emphasis to obtaining employment and cultivating a successful career. Chapter 5, "Gaining Employment I: Basic Considerations," scans the contemporary employment scene and highlights the growth in the numbers of psychologists. Consideration is given to job prospects (with emphasis on new roles), earlier and current role and service definitions, employment satisfaction, and how applicants are selected for employment. Recognizing discrimination and shifting priorities from political and public policy sources, it is acknowledged that employment selection and job possibilities occur today in a less than ideal set of circumstances. To be best prepared to enter and compete in the job market, prerequisites and specialty qualifications are identified.

With the present employment scene, it is essential to understand how applicants for positions are evaluated and chosen. Chapter 6, "Gaining Employment II: Understanding the Selection System," faces the reality of interdisciplinary competition, and clarifies how the applicant can obtain distinguishing qualifications (e.g., specialized credentials, memberships, and training). Facts and figures on employment opportunities and incomes are given.

Since clinical psychology has become a well developed and lucrative profession, there has been a significant increase in regulation of practitioners. Chapter 7, "Being Professional: Ethics and Law," is based on the fact that the degree of self-determination by the clinical psychologist has markedly changed and is being superseded by nonpsychological regulatory sources. Professional ethics and practice guidelines are of critical importance to the judgments made by the clinical psychologist, and are becoming more prescriptive and proscriptive. Many of these guidelines are by third-party payment sources, which elevate the importance of economics over quality care per se. Of greatest significance, there is an unprecedented degree of governmental regulation of the practice of clinical psychology, such as by state licensing boards and regulatory agencies; highly specific rules for practices are being promulgated without peer authority. This chapter reviews the various sources of regulation, and gives special emphasis to malpractice.

Before deciding to enter or remain in clinical psychology, the future must be appraised. Chapter 8, "The Future of Preparation and Employment in Clinical Psychology," notes self-defeating behavior that has occurred within the profession and reveals how to avoid it and remedy the consequences. Special emphasis is placed on governmental health care reform and commercial managed health care systems. Rather than considering these sources in a negative light, they should be viewed as opportunities. Recommendations are given about how trainers, students, and practitioners can adapt to the expectations of governmental and commercialized managed health care sources, and establish and maintain a successful career in clinical psychology. Contrary to the prophets of doom, the future of clinical psychology is bright.

In keeping with the evolution of professional psychology, the term *clinical psychology* is used in this book more to describe training, roles, competencies, skills, and services, as opposed to simply being used as the name of a training program in a university. The modern view is that clinical psychology may be properly provided by persons from other psychological specialties, particularly counseling and school psychology; and there is the option for a psychologist from a nonclinical specialty to augment his or her

credentials in order to move into clinical services. Therefore, the contents of this book are suited to training psychologists of every ilk, as well as mental health counselors,
marriage and family therapists, pastoral counselors, rehabilitation counselors, social workers, psychiatric nurses,
and medical physicians.

Robert Henley Woody
Malcolm Higgins Robertson

Chapter 1

History and Evolution I: From the Early Years to 1980

Preparing for and being employed in clinical psychology bring to mind the old adage, "You cannot understand the present without knowledge of the past." In contrast to certain other health care professions, the evolution of clinical psychology is remarkable; it must be recognized in order to form ideas about what might occur in the future. In other words, the mission of this book is to equip the reader to comprehend the factors that shape clinical psychology, be it past, present, or future. It is only through this sort of knowledge that wise decisions can be made about whether or not to dedicate one's life to a career in psychology.

1890–1910: THE BEGINNING

The history of clinical psychology encompasses approximately 100 years. In 1996, the profession celebrates its first centennial.

In the last decade of the nineteenth century, the profession of clinical psychology was launched by a few maverick psychologists who broke ranks with their scientific colleagues and left the hallowed laboratories of academe for an uncertain future in the marketplace. Before this time, scientific psychology was primarily the study of the elements of consciousness, and most psychologists were opposed to clinical applications (Reisman, 1981).

Shortly before 1900, the vision of a profession of psychology was articulated by Lightner Witmer who boldly proposed that psychologists use their knowledge and tools to improve the quality of life (Reisman, 1981, chapter 2). He spoke of a new profession, which he called clinical psychology, although the name had been used earlier in France in a general sense (Garfield, 1982).

In 1896, Witmer founded the first psychological clinic at the University of Pennsylvania. According to Witmer, the laboratory would be a clinic, with the tools being psychological tests; the subjects would be handicapped children; and the method would be a single-subject format based on the systematic administration and evaluation of tests. The practical value would be a remedial plan designed for each child; and the scientific value would be in the new knowledge derived from the cumulative findings of many single case studies. By 1904, James McKeen Cattell stated that psychology would be not only a science but also a profession (Cattell, 1937). In 1907, Witmer founded *The Psychological Clinic*, a journal for the profession of clinical psychology (Reisman, 1981, p. 6).

If Witmer's proposal struck a quixotic note at the time, his parochial statement that other professionals lacked the unique training of psychologists strained the credulity of even those sympathetic to his mission. Though the statement was one of high purpose, it was based on faith rather than fact—at that time no psychologist possessed the unique training endorsed by Witmer. The question of training aside, there was no one else doing what Witmer called on psychologists to do.

The response within psychology ranged from dismay to opposition. Except for a few colleagues of like mind, the response of the establishment was predictable: the proposal of psychology as a profession was a repudiation of psychology as a pure science; if taken seriously, it would be an irreversible setback. The implications of Witmer's proposal were not lost upon other professional groups. A goodly number of educators, social workers, and physicians viewed the move as a threat to their professional sovereignty. With some justification, they argued that psychologists lacked a professional identity in the public's eye.

Yet predictions of the profession's early demise never materialized. The belief that prevailed was that psychology could be, ought to be, and would be a profession. That belief was prophetic, and actually an underestimation of the future status that would be accorded to clinical psychology.

By 1910, five universities had clinics; three had some semblance of a professional training curriculum; and a forerunner of today's clinical psychology internship had been established by Henry Goddard at the Vineland Training Center in Vineland, New Jersey (Reisman, 1991, chapter 3). From that point on, clinical psychology never looked back.

1910–1930: THE EARLY YEARS

If the preceding 20 years might be characterized by a new breed of psychologist in search of a client population, the ensuing two decades could be characterized by a client population in search of the professional psychologist.

Two events contributed to the profession's gathering momentum. First was the strong demand for psychological testing and evaluation in schools and in the military service during World War I. Psychological tests were an efficient method of classifying the large number of military recruits. Educators also saw the value of psychological tests as a practical tool to assess intellectual growth and academic achievement in children. With the development of measures for intelligence, aptitudes, interests, and personality, psychological testing became commercially as well as professionally successful (Goldenberg, 1983, chapter 2). Second was the limited number of university programs to train psychological practitioners. In short, a fast growing need pressing against insufficient resources led inevitably to an upsurge in university-based clinics and training programs. By 1914, 19 universities had psychological clinics to train clinical psychologists and another 68 would be added over the next 20 years (Kirsch and Winter, 1983).

Increasing numbers of psychologists sought a career in the clinical practice of psychology, though at this time most of their training was learning by doing. Continued penetration of the human service area by psychologists (though limited to an educational–remedial focus), was coupled with the fact that they were being accorded legal status in some states and allowed to sit on commissions responsible for committing the retarded to institutions. Clinical psychologists were becoming a professional force.

As expected, opposition mounted both within and outside psychology. Some physicians contended that a lack of psychoanalytic training weakened psychologists' claims to clinical competence. Some educators were alarmed at the potential (and occasionally actual) abuse of tests. Some social workers found fault with the excessive reliance on diagnosis. Skeptical scientific colleagues decried the lack of experimental rigor in "clinical studies."

Wisely, clinical psychologists chose first to confront the opposition within their own ranks. Confident of a growing numerical strength, the profession executed a tour de force and in 1917, formed an independent American Association of Clinical Psychologists (AACP). The hand of the American Psychological Association (APA) was forced, and in the spirit of "divided we perish, united we stand," proffered an invitation to set up a clinical psychology section of APA with full rights and privileges. The AACP disbanded as precipitously as it had incorporated, and its members returned to the APA in 1919.

Flushed with its first political victory and buoyed by a newly acquired power base within APA, the clinical psychology section served notice that it would pursue parity both within and outside psychology. Top priority would be given to seeking a legal definition of professional psychology and to establishing university-based Ph.D. programs to train clinical psychologists.

At this juncture and as an aside, it is interesting to note that L. Crane (1925–1926) set forth an idea that was rejected then but has achieved professional fruition today. His idea was that there should be an exclusively professional training program with a doctor of psychology (Psy.D.) degree. His idea was not supported, and 40 years passed before a similar idea received a considered hearing within the APA.

Returning to the emergence of clinical psychology and its embrace by APA, scarcely 30 years had passed since the day that Lightner Witmer had presented his clinical psychology proposal at an APA meeting, and the words of Joseph Jastrow, one of psychology's most respected elder statesmen, had a prophetic ring: "Yet of all the applications, that of clinical psychology appears to me the most momentous" (Jastrow, 1930, cited in Reisman, 1991, p. 162).

1930–1940: THE TIME OF TRANSITION

As the twenties drew to a close, clinical psychologists faced a sharply curtailed job market due primarily to an economic depression, and secondarily to a still fuzzy notion of who was really a clinical psychologist. Nevertheless, the profession began the decade of the thirties on an upbeat note.

With an official section to represent its interests, clinical psychologists became a vocal, if small minority within APA. Approximately 20 percent of the APA membership listed clinical psychology as a research, teaching, or service interest (Goldenberg, 1983, chapter 2). Another statistic that seemed to bode well for the future was that some 40 percent of APA members had full-time employment outside academia. Although only one-fourth of this group were clinical practitioners, four times as many (those who could not or would not belong to APA) were doing clinical work. Reisman (1981) estimates that there were approximately 800 clinical psychologists at the beginning of the thirties, a number that would grow to nearly 30,000 by the end of the eighties. With the increasing emphasis on service delivery, the profession's academically derived identity had to be stretched to include the community centered practitioner.

With the worst of the Great Depression over and the job market brightening, clinicians began to take a close look at their role definition. Many felt boxed in by the traditional focus on the handicapped child. More importantly, they objected to a professional role that confined their practice to diagnosis and treatment planning. In short, they wanted another piece of the action, and the missing piece was treatment. After all, it was there in Witmer's blueprint—clinical psychologists would use their knowledge and methods to improve the quality of life, mentally, emotionally, and socially for individuals of all ages.

Opposition surfaced immediately and hewed pretty much to party lines. Psychiatrists quickly invoked the specter of charlatanism and admonished that, in addition to psychoanalytic training, a medical degree was the sine qua non for assuming full responsibility for the welfare of client/patients. Academic psychologists deplored yet another deviation from the strict canons of science. The conservative voices of the profession cautioned against rocking the boat by reaching for too much too soon.

The opposition was answered by a commitment to define standards of practice and establish accreditation procedures for training programs. In 1935, a hastily assembled APA Committee on Standards of Training (in a surprising display of collegial unanimity) reaffirmed the commitment to standards of practice and accreditation procedures. Next, the committee attempted to defuse opposition to the treatment issue by defining two levels of practitioners: a professional psychologist (doctorate and one year of supervised experience), and an assistant psychologist (master's and one year of supervised experience). The committee then capped off its work with the statement that was to be a harbinger of future controversy, namely, that clinical psychology is the *art* (a term that would require endless disclaimers), and *technology* (another term that would be disavowed again and again) which deals with adjustment problems of human beings (Reisman, 1991, pp. 210–211). It was all there, the polarization within the profession over subdoctoral training, the territorial dispute with psychiatry, the scientist–practitioner conundrum, and the rivalry between the technocratic practitioners and the humanistic practitioners. In a statement that foreshadowed the later rise of practitioner oriented degree programs, Louttit (1939) concluded:

> For a real professional dealing with problems of behavior, the future must produce a new specialist. This behavior specialist will be the product of an entirely new curriculum which will include pertinent materials from psychology, medicine, education, sociology and social work. It may even be necessary to establish a new degree as a symbol of the curriculum [p. 384, quoted in Garfield, 1992, pp. 9–10].

Although supported by APA's Committee on Standards, the clinical section of APA chafed under the slow-moving parent organization. So in 1937, the clinicians left APA to join the American Association of Applied Psychologists (AAAP) (Reisman, 1991, chapter 6). Despite the developing factionalism, by the end of the thirties clinical psychologists could take some pride in their contribution to diagnostic testing, which now encompassed psychopathology as well as the earlier achievements in intellectual, educational, and vocational assessment.

1940–1950: THE EXPANSION YEARS

In the 1940s, a new dimension was added to the growth of clinical psychology. As Sterling (1982) aptly put it, "Affluence pushed its nose under our tent" (p. 789). As might be expected, affluence created new problems about as fast as it solved old ones. But in the beginning and for some time after, it was a heady experience.

In recognition of the significant contributions made by clinical psychologists during World War II, the Veterans Administration (VA) turned to psychology for assistance in providing service to veterans who were psychiatric casualties. The VA alone required 4700 clinical psychologists (Goldenberg, 1983, chapter 2).

The profession was faced with the enviable problem of how to use the federal government's largesse to alleviate the shortage of training programs and trained practitioners. In 1944, a joint committee of APA and AAAP (the latter ended their walk-out a year later and returned to the fold) agreed to use VA, U.S. Department of Public Health (USDPH), and National Institute of Mental Health (NIMH) funds to expand already existing graduate facilities.

During this period the visibility of the profession rose dramatically. Undergraduate and graduate enrollments soared, and psychology departments were rapidly expanded by students drawn to a field that offered an oversupply of jobs, attractive salaries, the excitement of doing psychotherapy, and for those who made it all the way, the status of a practitioner with a doctoral degree.

Between 1946 and 1949, the number of doctoral clinical psychology programs rose from 22 to 42, and by the end of the decade approximately 60 doctoral programs were training close to 1500 clinical graduate students (Kirsch and Winter, 1983), but applications still far outnumbered available spaces.

In 1947, the APA Committee on Training in Clinical Psychology, which was responsible for specifying curriculum content, setting standards of training, and placing its imprimatur on doctoral programs that met the standards, became alarmed at the prospect of the "clinical tail wagging the scientific dog." With the hope of striking an optimal balance between scientific and professional education, the APA formed a committee, chaired by David Shakow, to set forth guidelines for graduate training in clinical psychology (Shakow, Hilgard, Kelly, Luckey, Sanford, and Shaffer, 1947). Two years later, the historic Boulder Conference, a summit meeting of leading clinical psychology educators, was held to plan implementation of the Shakow Report. The intent was to close the schism between science and the profession. The conference mandated that a clinical psychologist be trained as a scientist and a practitioner in graduate, as opposed to professional, schools (Raimy, 1950). Then, with a passing reference to the need for innovative programming, the conference reaffirmed the existing Ph.D. model, in which the first and fourth years were set aside for scientific instruction and the second and third years for the professional program. Frank (1984) states that the emphasis on research training was designed to give clinical psychologists an independence from psychiatrists in clinical settings.

With the AAAP and two other separatist organizations reuniting with APA in 1945 (Frank, 1984), the discipline appeared to have resolved its internal politics. Wolfe (1946) captured the spirit of accord with the statement that "the object of the APA should be to advance Psychology as a science, as a profession, and as a means of promoting human welfare" (p. 3). At this juncture, clinical and counseling practitioners accounted for almost half of the psychology positions outside academia; salaries of doctoral clinicians had nearly doubled; the clinical division of APA now accounted for about 20 percent of the total membership (not counting a sizable number of associate members); and slightly more than 50 percent of those affiliated with

APA expressed an interest in professional applications (Reisman, 1991).

Although the practice of psychotherapy loomed as a potentially divisive issue among psychologists, psychiatry's opposition helped to close ranks, and APA's policy was that psychotherapy had a legitimate place in the training and practice of clinical psychologists. Besides, by the beginning of World War II nearly one-third of all clinical psychologists included psychotherapy in their practice (Kirsch and Winter, 1983).

Although two states, Connecticut and Virginia, had passed certification laws for doctoral clinical psychologists, APA decided that the matter was too critical to be left entirely to the states. First, it could not be assumed that states would follow suit, or that standards would necessarily be uniform. With that in mind, the American Board of Examiners in Professional Psychology (ABEPP) was founded to provide national certification for the specialties of clinical, counseling, and industrial psychology.

The profession's strong suit was still assessment and diagnosis, though a healthy skepticism had taken hold, especially in response to the unfavorable research reviews of projective techniques (non- or semistructured test stimuli to which clients respond). The profession moved to loosen psychiatry's proprietary control of psychotherapy. The pioneering work of Carl R. Rogers (1942) not only gave psychologists a psychotherapy theory of their own, but also ushered in a period of productive research on the effect of different treatment procedures.

1950–1960: THE PERIOD OF CONSOLIDATION

The demand for clinical psychology was still strong and it had become the largest APA division. The number of APA-approved doctoral programs continued to grow. Close to half the psychology Ph.D.s graduated in clinical psychology

(Goldenberg, 1983, chapter 2). As a reflection of the mounting concern over the rapid growth of clinical training programs, two summit conferences on professional education and training were held within a three-year period, the Stanford Conference in 1955 and the Miami Conference in 1958.

During this period, 13 more states wrote certification laws. The American Psychiatric Association first offered and then withdrew its support of psychologist certification. This reversal may have been triggered by the portents riding on a Michigan State Supreme Court ruling that a clinical psychologist could serve as an expert witness in a determination of mental illness (Reisman, 1991, chapter 8).

About this time, the ABPP (the E had since been dropped) had 1403 duly certified diplomates, two-thirds of whom were clinical psychologists. Early on, APA preferred certification (i.e., qualified to use the title of psychologist) to licensing (i.e., qualified to practice psychology) to avoid premature definition of a practitioner's role, and to sidestep conflict with other mental health professions. It also encouraged voluntary rather than mandatory certification so as not to give the appearance of discriminating against nonclinically trained psychologists.

The profession reaffirmed its commitment to develop the area of psychotherapy. In addition to Carl Rogers' (1942, 1951) seminal ideas, a systematic blending of learning principles and psychodynamic concepts was being fashioned by several psychologists, notably John Dollard and Neal Miller (1950). As was true of psychodiagnosis, the first rush of enthusiasm was now tempered by skepticism over uncritical claims of success rates for psychotherapy.

Mindful of its responsibility to uphold the integrity of the discipline and to safeguard the welfare of society, APA promulgated its first code of professional ethics in 1951. Then, to show that scientific and professional psychology were compatible, APA chose two eminent scientist-practitioners, first Carl Rogers and then Paul Meehl, to receive the Gold Medal Award for significant contributions to the science of psychology.

1960–1970: THE TIME OF CONFLICT AND GROWTH

If the fifties were the halcyon years, the sixties was a more complex decade. There were 35,000 psychologists (APA membership was 27,000, compared to 31 members at its inauguration in 1892), one-third of whom identified themselves as clinical psychologists (Reisman, 1991, chapter 9). The number of Ph.D.-approved programs had almost tripled since the forties, and all but three states had statutory certification. Generous grants were still available for training and research, and funds continued to flow from the federal coffers.

The priorities accorded to mental health programs by the Kennedy and Johnson administrations were not always executed in a perfect fashion. For example, some training programs occasionally received more federal dollars than they could spend, and would aggressively recruit trainees, sometimes lowering their admission standards, rather than turning "money back to the Feds." It was, of course, this faulty administration of funds that, quite justly, produced lasting public policy criticism and suspicion about funding training in the mental health professions.

In the sixties, employers bid competitively with each other to fill newly created clinical psychology positions. Graduate students were hired at both doctoral and master's levels almost immediately following (and sometimes before) graduation. It was common for a new graduate to have numerous job offers from which to choose. Incidentally, this fertile job market extended on to the universities, as graduate programs expanded rapidly, leading to new faculty positions. It was an era when a clinical psychologist could readily receive better offers; as a result, there was considerable job mobility.

Even factoring in new graduate programs and the expansion of existing ones, manpower shortages were projected to rise sharply at national, state, and local levels. Noteworthy is L. Wright's (1983) observation that in the late 1960s there were seven positions for every clinical psychology graduate compared to a 1:1 ratio in the 1980s.

On the other hand, the issue of the conflicting priorities of a science and a profession were still unresolved. Garfield (1966) spoke of clinical psychology's "dual identity of a science and a profession as a source of uniqueness and enrichment, as well as a source of divisiveness and discontent" (p. 353). Garfield then went on to say:

> In less than 20 years we have witnessed and experienced the following: increased professionalization and concern with professional problems, increased demands for our services with accompanying social rewards, an emphasis on state certification and licensing, the setting up of formal training programs in clinical psychology, a broadening of professional roles, an increase in private practice, a decline in traditional testing, a marked emphasis on psychotherapy, increased disharmony between the science and profession of psychology, and some evidence of dissatisfaction among those in the profession [p. 354].

In effect the discipline of psychology had two masters, one with power and the other with money, and each threatened the other's vested interests. The pure science faction resented the money being put into strictly professional pursuits, and charged that professional concerns preempted the training of clinical psychology students. Those on the professional (clinical) side of the aisle felt shortchanged in terms of influence and control within APA, as they discovered that a majority of numbers did not equate with majority clout.

A few prestigious departments summarily dropped their clinical programs. A separatist group, the Psychonomic

Society, was organized for the pursuit of psychology as a pure science; and in 1960 held its first meeting at the University of Chicago. Some clinical programs were transferred to colleges of education and medicine. In professional circles talk was heard of leaving APA to form an independently funded organization that would put the full force of its resources behind the promotion of psychology as a profession (a maneuver that had been successful twice before). From both sides came suggestions that APA be split into separate organizations, each free to pursue its priorities. Albee (1970) proposed an American Scientific Psychological Association and an American Professional Psychological Association coexisting side by side.

To stem the tide of the separatist movement and to cool down the in-house feuding, the National Conference on the Professional Preparation of Clinical Psychologists was held in Chicago in 1965. Its purpose was to redress the complaints of the practitioner group without subverting the Boulder model of the scientist-practitioner. The recommendations for more and different professional preparation were largely ignored, even though implicit in the Boulder legacy was permission to experiment with training models.

As with the two previous conferences held in the fifties, there was struggle between those who supported the current Boulder model but with additional professional training, and others who wanted major changes in the education of clinicians. As chairman of the 1965 APA Committee on Scientific and Professional Aims, Kenneth Clark made a plea for a practitioner-oriented training program that would grant a Psy.D. degree. Three years later, with support from several APA divisions, state psychological associations, and professional societies, the National Council on Graduate Education in Psychology endorsed Clark's proposal (Caddy, 1981). It was an idea whose time had come, although Crane (1925–1926), Poffenberger (1938), and Louttit (1939) had proposed alternative degree programs for clinicians in previous decades, and Gardner in the forties had proposed a School of Professional Psychology (Harrower, 1947).

By the end of the sixties, two solutions were in place: The first, and the first officially endorsed Psy.D. program, was a two-track system at the University of Illinois (Peterson, 1968). One track was the traditional Ph.D. with primary emphasis on developing research and teaching skills; the other was a Psy.D. with primary emphasis on teaching clinical skills, with applications to either program filtered through the same stringent admission criteria. The other solution was the California School of Professional Psychology's six-year career ladder divided into four degree rungs (A.A., B.A., M.A., and Ph.D.), with admission criteria that considered personal suitability as well as academic aptitude.

With its corporate image burnished by a new eight-story headquarters building in Washington, DC, APA stood ready to lend its skill bank and resources to solving the great social problems of the sixties: racism, poverty, over-population, and the assault on society's traditions by an alienated and disenchanted youth.

Within the mental health community, clinical psychology had effected a rapprochement with allied professions through membership in interdisciplinary organizations coupled with a wider participation in the delivery of mental health services. Indicative of an advancing professional maturity was the expansion of both predoctoral and post-doctoral opportunities for specialty concentrations, such as clinical, counseling, child clinical, clinical–community psychology, and subspecialty areas such as neuropsychological assessment, forensic psychology, crisis intervention, group therapy, and marital–family therapy.

For many (perhaps most) in the profession, the high point of this decade was the community mental health movement, which Hobbs (1964) called the third revolution, the first being humane treatment of the insane and the second belonging to Freud. What the grants from VA, NIMH, and USDPH did for professional education in the forties and fifties, the infusion of federal monies into the country's mental health system did for career opportunities and advancement in the sixties. For the client population the salutary effect was a significant expansion of publicly supported mental health services at the community level. As a consequence, services were made available for a broader spectrum of psychological disorders, and the more seriously disturbed persons could be treated in their own community as an alternative to being isolated in an institution.

With the progress of the preceding twenty years, clinical psychology was in a good position to take advantage of the windfall created by nationwide funding for the construction and implementation of comprehensive mental health centers (CMHC). Salaries and career benefits improved to keep pace with the rising shortage of mental health professionals to staff the newly created CCMHs. Within the centers, the broad spectrum of mental health services created diversification in terms of job opportunities. Those with a strong clinical bent could hone their diagnostic and therapeutic skills; clinical–community psychologists were phased into prevention, consultation, and education; research skills were needed for program evaluation; others with managerial and organizational talents could find positions in administration and program development; and the pedagogically inclined found opportunities for the supervision of psychology trainees and paraprofessionals.

Funds from the Community Mental Health Centers Act (1963) not only made mental health services more accessible, but also provided new services, such as partial hospitalization, crisis intervention, and consultation and education (Bellak and Hersen, 1980). The CMHCs also gave an impetus to experimenting with brief or time-limited forms of therapy, as well as the development of new treatment approaches, such as existential, gestalt, behavioral, rational-emotive, and transactional analysis.

However, during this period, clinical research studies repeatedly demonstrated that the value of diagnostic and therapeutic techniques left much to be desired (Garfield, 1966). Albee (1970) observed that: "professional ingenuity in inventing new forms of psychotherapy has at least kept pace with the efforts of evaluators to catch up and expose it" (p. 1075). Furthermore, the enthusiasm and pride that accompanied formation of national certification through ABPP had waned, and applications to all the specialty areas had trailed off noticeably. A survey by Robyak and Goodyear (1984) disclosed that the largest percentage of ABPP diplomates in clinical psychology graduated in the fifties. The rapid formation of state certification provided a means of obtaining credentials that, in contrast to ABPP, had legal status, grass roots relevancy, less rigorous preparation, and were less expensive.

In addition, discouragement persisted over the failure to loosen the grip of the medical model (which viewed psychological disorder as an illness) on the thinking of mental health professionals, including many clinical psychologists (Albee, 1966–1967). Despite being the only human service profession to combine a science of human behavior with a professional discipline, psychology continued to come up short against a model whose credibility rested largely on metaphor and analogy.

Also, there was the unsettling discrepancy between what clinical psychologists were supposed to be and what in fact they did. Although trained as scientist-practitioners, the large majority of clinicians wanted to be doctor-practitioners rather than doctor-scientists. (As Katkin [1982] notes, the scientist–practitioner model may be pronounced with a silent "scientist.") Such clinicians could talk knowledgeably about research, but they seldom did it and rarely published. Graduate clinical psychology programs simply failed to instill the sense of excitement necessary to doing

research (Strupp, 1982). In practice, the modus operandi
of the Ph.D. clinical psychologist differed only slightly
from, on the one hand, that of the more highly paid psychiatrist, and on the other, the psychiatric social worker
with much less training. Although the Ph.D. clinician was
gaining parity with psychiatrists by having therapeutic
and managerial responsibilities commensurate with professional training, de facto discrimination was still evident
in both salary and administrative authority.

The definitional problem was also played out in the
graduate schools, where clinical psychology students
learned to finesse their ways through the often conflicting requirements of the scientific and professional program components. Meanwhile, George Albee (1966–1967)
was warning that in 10 to 20 years most clinical psychologists would be leaving the CMHCs for university teaching or the private sector.

1970–1980: THE MATURING YEARS

Clinical psychology began the seventies with a quarter of
a century of rapid and healthy growth behind it. Much that
transpired in the 1970s had to do with improving the
image of clinical psychology and enlarging the scope of
clinical practice. A convincing case had to be made to the
sister professions (psychiatry, psychiatric nursing, and
social work), legislative bodies, and the public at large that
the clinical psychologist was not a technician who only administered diagnostic tests, but was an independently
functioning, professionally accountable practitioner. What
followed was a deemphasis on diagnostic testing in favor
of therapeutic interventions. Kelly (1961) pointed to a shift
in this direction beginning in the late fifties, and Cleveland (1976) cites several cogent reasons for the decline of
diagnostic testing.

In the seventies, a typical distribution of a Ph.D.
clinician's time was 50 percent therapy, 20 percent

assessment-diagnosis, 20 percent supervision-consultation, and 10 percent administration. Another part of upgrading the image was to point out that a clinical psychologist worked not only as a salaried public servant, but also as a private, fee-for-service provider. In fact, psychologists were penetrating the private sector in larger numbers than ever before. Approximately 40 percent of clinicians were engaged in some private practice, and the number of practitioners available for private practice was fast approaching that of psychiatrists, but with a better geographic spread (Dorken, 1977).

Within psychology, it was necessary to correct the notion that clinical work was more art than science. A positive step in this direction was a shift from all-purpose, a priori based tests to empirically derived, specifically targeted assessments, such as neuropsychological measures and behavior rating scales. In psychotherapy research, close attention was paid to tailoring therapeutic interventions to the specific problems of clients and patients. Another ameliorative change was the turning away from the image of the clinician as a generalist to the image of a specialist, for example, forensic psychologist, child psychologist, marriage and family psychologist, medical psychologist, or clinical neuropsychologist.

The penetration of the private sector was facilitated by the rise in third-party payments to psychologists for mental health services. At both federal and state levels, restrictions were being lifted on the public's access to psychologists. By the late seventies, 35 states and Washington, DC, encompassing 78 percent of the population, had enacted statutes providing access to and free choice of a licensed or certified psychologist for covered mental health benefits (C. Levy, 1981). In addition, efforts were being made to include clinical psychologists in Medicare and Medicaid.

Behind every successful profession is a strong lobby that can promote political, social, and economic advancement.

In 1974, the APA established its first advocacy organization, the Association for the Advancement of Psychology (AAP), to foster the interests of professional psychology. Dorken (1979) comments, "as it has been said, the price of success is eternal vigilance—and a damned good lobby" (p. 17). Precedents had been set 40 years earlier by the formation of the Psychologists League, a professional lobby group to assist unemployed psychologists and to prod the federal government into greater utilization of psychologists (Machover, 1980), and earlier in this decade in the formation of the Council for the Advancement of the Psychological Professions and Sciences (CAPPS) (Wright, 1992).

By the midseventies, with the exception of Missouri, all states and Washington, DC, had either licensing or certification statutes that covered over 25,000 psychologists (Dorken, 1977). The growth of the private practice model underscored the importance of having professional credentials defined by licensure rather than certification, to be licensed to practice in preference to a certified professional title. Consequently, at the state level the profession began a drive to replace certification with licensure.

The accountability ethic also loomed large during this period. Plans were drawn up to implement the concept of peer reviews of clinical practice in both the public and private sectors. Access to information on qualified psychologists was sorely needed by referral sources and third-party payers. The answer was forthcoming in the publication of the National Register of Health Service Providers, a voluntary, peer-reviewed listing of psychological practitioners. By the 1980s over 13,000 psychologists would be listed (McConnell, 1984). To combat the "half-life" of professional knowledge (Dubin, 1972), a strong campaign was started to encourage practitioners to obtain continuing professional education. Finally, the APA Council of Representatives commissioned the Committee on Standards for Providers for Psychological Services to begin work on developing both generic and special standards for training and practice in the applied areas of clinical, counseling, school, and industrial–organizational psychology (Barron, 1977–1978).

An issue of pivotal significance in the seventies was whether a clinical psychologist would continue to be defined as a mental health specialist who dealt exclusively with psychological disorders, or as a primary health care professional who dealt with both physical and psychological disorders. The issue had strong currency at the time because of several critical trends, the first of which was the shift of medical education and practice from a biological disease model to a comprehensive psychosocial model, in which the focus was on the patient with the illness rather than the illness per se (Schneider, 1980). The second trend was the anticipated arrival of National Health Insurance (NHI). The uncertainty over whether NHI would include mental health benefits gave a special urgency to broadening the definition of the clinical psychologist as a health care provider. More immediate was the formation of health maintenance organizations (HMOs), an alternative to the private insurer/private practitioner arrangement, that tailored their programs to an emphasis on prevention of illness and fostering healthy living habits. With its relatively short history in delivery of professional services, clinical psychology had the flexibility to adapt to the new concept. The third issue was the promotion of a healthy life-style as a significant social movement, supported by the concern of government and industry over the enormous expenditures on medical care, as well as the general public's heightened consciousness of and commitment to healthy living. Fourth was the perception that health maintenance and prevention of illness was an area largely unattended to by other professions, and one that presented psychology with an opportunity to be in the vanguard of the movement through research, education, and service.

Over the years, an increasing number of clinical psychologists had plied their trade within hospitals, medical

schools, and family and pediatric medical settings. From
this natural base, they could now expand their traditional
role to assess the psychological antecedents and consequences of physical illness and disease, and to assist patients to participate in their own recovery by replacing
unhealthy living habits with healthy coping behaviors
(Schneider, 1980). Schofield (1969) summoned clinical
psychologists to the challenge by contrasting their role as
mental health professionals in the past, and the opportunity now for a larger role in the health sciences with
emphasis on a broader spectrum of human behavior. Following Schofield's summons, the APA Board of Scientific
Affairs appointed a task force to study and make recommendations for psychology as a health care profession
(Matarazzo, 1980). Shortly thereafter, a new APA division,
the Division of Health Psychology, was established. Several universities began doctoral programs in health psychology or behavioral medicine. Behavioral health internships
were soon established. Health psychology was finding a
place in the traditional clinically oriented curriculum.

Besides strengthening psychology's long-time interface with medicine, health psychology had a unifying impact within psychology. The focus on nonclinical as well
as clinical populations, and the need for research and education as well as service, created a common pathway for
both the scientists and the professionals. Having overcome
much of the earlier opposition from the traditionalists, behavioral clinical psychologists, with their strong suit of
helping clients learn and unlearn overt habit patterns,
were emerging as the cutting edge of the development of
a health care profession.

Psychology's commitment to capture a broader employment market was taking place against a backdrop of
shrinking job opportunities in higher education and mental health (APA, 1975) caused by the national recession
in the early 1970s. The scarcity of teaching and research
positions led many nonclinical Ph.D.s to seek employment

in areas of higher demand. Some surveys showed that psychology trainers had created an oversupply of candidates; there were perhaps a twofold greater number of candidates than professional manpower needs or societal demand (Balch and Harper, 1976). Albee (1977) predicted hard times for psychologists, with Ph.D.s entering the armed forces in unprecedented numbers. Graduate students were feeling the economic crunch. Financial support had fallen off sharply, even as the number of applications continued to increase. Although there were 100 APA-approved clinical programs (a fivefold increase in 25 years), the large number of applicants relative to available space produced a selection ratio of 3 to 5 percent for APA-approved programs which was more competitive than that of most medical schools (Nyman, 1973).

As an aside, it seems appropriate to acknowledge that most, if not all, trainers were aware of the diminishing job market and abundance of candidates for positions. Nonetheless, they chose to keep admissions high and to continue to produce the same or a greater number of clinical psychologists as in the past. Certain critics would allege that this overadmission policy, which regrettably continues to this day in some training facilities, had a less than honorable motive, namely to preserve the employment of the existing faculty and the budgets of their academic units.

Returning to the recession in the early 1970s and the decline in employment opportunities, graduate programs continued to turn out as many master's level psychologists as ever. With their lower salary demands, they posed a competitive threat to both Ph.D. clinicians and nonclinical Ph.D.s who were moving into the service area. In addition, opposition from insurance companies and the medical profession to reimbursing psychologists singled out the subdoctoral status of the master's level psychologist. Some Ph.D. private practitioners perceived the master's level clinician as a hindrance to their efforts to jockey for a more favorable position in the fee-for-service market (Havens, 1979). Furthermore, with considerable money and prestige at stake if NHI became a reality, many in the profession were willing to jettison the subdoctoral degree if it proved to be a roadblock to psychology's inclusion in NHI.

Master's practitioners were encountering concerted opposition to statutory recognition at the state level. Both the ABPP and the APA Council of Representatives were on record against continuing the terminal master's degree (a consolation prize for those who failed to pass through to subdoctoral status), and the latter argued that only doctoral practitioners could function independently or call themselves "psychologists" (Havens, 1979). The objections were the familiar ones of limited competency and lack of uniform training standards, and though the objections were usually accompanied by proposals to upgrade master's level training, few were ever acted on.

The APA's Education and Training Board, while acknowledging the economic competition, sustained its support of master's level training. In 1973, the conference on Levels and Patterns of Professional Training in Psychology took place at Vail, Colorado (Korman, 1974) and singled out the contributions of the subdoctoral psychologist to the nation's mental health manpower force (Dimond, Havens, Rathnow, and Colliver, 1977), as had each of the three earlier conferences on professional training. But the Vail Conference went one step further with a proposal of a career lattice for the master's practitioner that would provide a framework for horizontal and vertical movement (Dimond et al., 1977).

Besides support from the education and training board and the welcomed affirmation of the Vail Conference, the master's group had some strong cards of its own. First, on the state level they were solidly entrenched in the mental health system, largely because they had been available to take up the slack created earlier by the shortage of Ph.D.s.

Second, threatened with professional extinction, the master's group had begun to organize, and with their sheer numbers they now posed a political threat at the state level.

The ongoing debate to reaffirm or not to reaffirm the Boulder model of scientist first and practitioner second appeared to be favoring the "negative" team. The 1973 Vail Conference first affirmed the merits of the scientist-practitioner model as exemplified in the traditional Ph.D. degree, and second, recommended a separate professional model to be designated by the Psy.D. degree (McConnell, 1984).

Gordon Derner, a distinguished trainer of clinical psychologists, had used the term *scholar-professional* to describe the model of training that is primarily practitioner oriented (Bellak and Hersen, 1980). This break with the traditional stance of previous conferences did not so much set forth new policy as it made existing policy congruent with reality. A forceful statement from *The Revolution in Professional Training* (Matulef, Pottharst, and Rothenberg, 1970) speaks to the growing dissatisfaction with traditional training.

> There is a revolution in professional training. Professional psychologists in all areas of institutional and private practice have united to change traditional and destructive training practices of many training programs. It is obvious now that what originally was a noble dream to unite science and practice within the same graduate student has now become a nightmare and a totally inadequate system for training professional psychologists [p. 1, quoted in Fox and Barclay, 1989, p. 57].

In 1973, the Psy.D. program at the University of Illinois (since discontinued) received APA accreditation. Before long, five new Psy.D. programs were in place and two additional schools of psychology. By the end of the 1970s, professional programs and schools of psychology were averaging 91 students per program compared to an average of 58 in the APA accredited scientist-practitioner programs (Caddy, 1981).

In 1978, the Virginia Beach Conference was convened to work out the specifics of the professional model endorsed by the Vail Conference, and to address the concerns over the proliferation of free-standing schools of psychology (Caddy, 1981). Internship directors had long faulted graduate programs for turning out inadequately trained clinical psychology interns. Part of the weak preparation could be traced to the traditional academic reward system that placed higher priority on research productivity than on training students. Frank (1984) refers to the lack of professional role models for graduate students because universities wanted scientists and not tradespeople on their faculties. The alternative professional programs would correct the bias by rewarding clinical faculty for time spent on training.

On balance, much had been accomplished in the seventies. The profession had gained considerable credibility with its sister health and human services professions, legislative bodies, and the public at large. The rift between science and the profession showed signs of healing. Between 1970 and 1980, four of the ten presidents of the APA were clinical psychologists (Reisman, 1981). Noteworthy is a statement in 1973 by Donald Campbell, "relating the practice of Psychology to the science of Psychology will continue to be an organizational [in contrast to being a philosophical] problem for APA." This statement on issues facing psychology appeared on the APA Election Ballot in 1973 when Campbell was President-Elect.

A survey of graduates between 1968 and 1980 from 80 accredited clinical psychology doctoral programs (S. F. Schneider, 1981) disclosed several sanguine trends: the percentage of minorities, especially women, had increased substantially; children's services were on the upswing; an intrapsychic orientation had given way to other approaches, such as community, marital-family, group, behaviorism, and humanism; there was virtually no unemployment; and the relevant question for graduates "[was] not whether psychology is a profession, but what kind of profession it wants to be" (p. 1445). Certainly, clinical psychology met the definition of a profession as set forth by Peterson (1976); namely, a set of techniques derived from a science or theory and applied differently to different problems, a professional society with membership based mainly on competence, and a code of ethics to safeguard the welfare of society.

However, the profession was guilty of footdragging in its response to advocacy for all types of minorities and the powerless, particularly mental patients confined to inadequately funded facilities with degrading living conditions and inadequate treatment programs. Simon (1975) asked for an advocate–professional model as a supplement to the scientist–professional model, and notes that psychologists have been preoccupied with their own professional minority concerns. Albee (1970) called on the profession to assume some responsibility for developing public awareness and then public support for intervention with the real problems of society; for example, racism, sexism, and economic exploitation.

Another issue that needed resolution was whether clinical psychologists would continue to operate in medicine, law, education, and industry, where they do not have squatters' rights, or build their own "house of business," as Albee had suggested in the 1965 Chicago Conference (McConnell, 1984).

Basically, clinical psychologists had gone where the demand was, and in doing so they frequently incurred an adoptive status. Something was clearly wrong when the only human service profession to have its own science of behavior, and to offer more innovative concepts and methods than other professions, had to spend inordinate time and energy gaining favor and fending off an adjunctive role. Whether clinical psychology can live outside its own sphere and still be recognized as an autonomous profession is a significant part of the unfinished business for the present and future. It was now the eve of the modern era for clinical psychology.

Chapter 2

History and Evolution II: The Mature Years, 1980 to the Mid-1990s

After some childlike growth spurts and an adolescentlike search for identity, the profession of psychology entered maturity. The period from 1980 to 1990 might well be characterized as stability versus change. Since 1990, the profession has achieved, without doubt, adulthood in the family of health care professions. Among the mental health professions, some might assert that psychology is the head of the household.

1980 TO 1990: STABILITY VERSUS CHANGE

Altman (1987), in his oft-cited treatise on centripetal and centrifugal phenomena in the evolution of the science and profession of psychology, characterizes the post-1960 period as primarily centrifugal (e.g., diverging, divisive, innovative, and change-based) in contrast to the centripetal (e.g., consolidating, unifying, insular, and change-resistant) delineation of the 1900 to 1960 period. An interesting refinement the author makes is that the two types of phenomena are not mutually exclusive; instead, they are like polar opposites that over time wax and wane in strength in relation to each other.

It may stretch Altman's thesis to characterize the previous decade as more centripetal than centrifugal (i.e., more emphasis on consolidating clinical psychology's already favorable image within and outside psychology than on staking a claim to new areas in which to practice). On the other hand, the decade of the 1980s clearly had a more centrifugal than centripetal look insofar as there was steady pressure to enlarge the scope of health care practice and to expand the practitioner's hegemony within the American Psychological Association. In fact, clinical psychology's commitment in the 1980s to expand and diversify exemplifies an axiom of the marketplace, to wit, if you're not moving ahead, you're falling behind. Or, perhaps it is a fact of competitive life not to let down or become complacent when you have momentum. That notion will become apparent in the legislative struggles and political victories and near victories discussed later in the chapter.

A survey of a significant subset of clinical psychologists (APA's Division of Clinical Psychology members) by Norcross, Prochaska, and Gallagher (1989a,b) found that on the average their sample respondents reported a reasonably high level of satisfaction with both their training and career choice (1989a); that psychotherapy occupied more time than any other professional activity (1989b), as was true in the previous decade; that assessment-diagnosis ranked second in the amount of professional time allotted (1989b) (note that the decline reported in the previous two decades seemed to have leveled off); and that compared to other survey data, research involvement and community consultation showed noticeable increases (1989b). Finally, Norcross et al. point to the continued rapid growth in private practice with upwards of 75 percent of psychologists engaged in full- or part-time fee for service work (1989a), a figure that would be even higher were nonmembers of the division included. In fact, the division of the Independent Practice of Psychology has become the third largest APA division (Walfish and Coovert, 1989).

Compared to other APA divisions, clinical psychology continues to maintain its preeminence in terms of sheer size and diversity of practice, and remains the largest division of APA. Slightly more than half of all psychology professionals report clinical psychology as their specialty field (Stapp, Tucker, and VandenBos, 1985). By 1989, 150 clinical psychology doctoral programs had received APA accreditation, half again as many as there were at the end of the previous decade. Moreover, clinical psychology comprises approximately 40 percent of all psychology doctorates awarded each year, with slightly more than one half of the clinical doctorates awarded to women (Strickland, 1985). For whatever reason, women made more rapid strides in their representation within the profession than ethnic minorities. Over the decade of the eighties, approximately 10 to 12 percent of clinical psychology doctorates were awarded annually to ethnic minorities, and approximately 5 percent of ethnic minorities were engaged in the professional practice of psychology (Hammond and Yung, 1993).

Although employment prospects for clinical psychologists in the late 1970s had rebounded from the recession in the earlier part of the decade, another recession in the early 1980s led to a shrinking job market in both higher education and mental health's public sector. Offsetting the economic downturn in higher education and mental health were two trends from the previous decade. Recall that an issue of pivotal significance in the 1970s was whether clinical psychologists would continue to define themselves as mental health specialists or opt (as many were and still are doing) for a broader (and certainly more marketable) definition of health care specialist. In short, the profession was able to use the greater diversity of career options that health psychology generated and the promising interface with inpatient and outpatient general health care to offset a declining job market in mental health's public sector. The other robust trend was the increased penetration of mental health's private practice sector which experienced much less of an economic downturn than did the public sector.

TRAINING AND EDUCATION MODELS

The scientist–practitioner model has been effectively matched by the practitioner–professional model. Strickland (1983a) estimated that practitioner programs account for over 25 percent of the clinical doctorates. Cummings (1984) predicted that within 10 years the majority of clinical psychologists would be trained in professional schools; in fact, a survey by Peterson and Stricker (1986) found that professional schools already accounted for more than 50 percent of those seeking a doctorate.

For the most part, however, the shift to practitioner-oriented programs had taken place outside universities. The large majority of graduate departments had not seen fit to adopt the recommendations of the Vail Conference and continued to endorse the Boulder training model of scientist–practitioner for Ph.D. and M.A. clinical programs (O'Sullivan and Quevillon, 1992). Perhaps these departments had heeded the implicit warning in APA's 1979 official reendorsement of the scientist–practitioner model.

APA's 1979 pronouncement favoring the scientist–practitioner model could be viewed as confirmation that the historical schism between science and the profession is still alive, well, and residing as always in a discipline deeply rooted in scholarly and scientific traditions. However, APA's position is also pragmatic, based on the alarming increase of free-standing schools of psychology that with few exceptions were unable or unwilling to affiliate with universities or already established university-based professional schools.

Basically, the issue is quality control (i.e., control over the quality of clinical students selected, trained, and graduated). Without the safeguards of a university setting, the threat of "counterfeit training" looms large. For many, the question is no longer whether to have Psy.D. practitioner programs, but how to ensure a strong connection with the scientific base of the profession. Efforts toward a rapprochement between the two professional training models were made in the late 1980s. National training conferences sponsored by those committed to preserve the scientist–practitioner model (Utah Conference, 1987; Gainesville Conference, 1990), and those advocating for the practitioner–professional school model (Mission Bay Conference, 1986; San Antonio Conference, 1990) have joined hands in endorsing an integration of science and practice. However, the endorsement is achieved by agreeing to a definition of science that is broader than the traditional one of conducting and publishing research, namely, to maintain a scientifically based attitude toward one's professional work.

Reflecting on the national training conferences held in the 1980s, Fox and Barclay (1989) conclude that: (1) there are, and will continue to be for the foreseeable future, three models of professional education and training, namely, a general education model in psychology as a core, the scientist–practitioner model, and the professional practitioner model; (2) that regardless of training model the education of clinical psychologists in the future will most likely take place in university affiliated settings; (3) doctoral graduates will be eligible for immediate licensure; and (4) training programs will prepare graduates to work effectively within a multicultural, pluralistic nation. Finally, contrary to earlier predictions, by 1990 it became apparent that the rapid growth rate of Psy.D. graduates in the late 1970s and early 1980s had slowed noticeably (Ellis, 1992) and Psy.D. programs account for less than one half of clinical doctorates (Shapiro and Wiggins, 1994).

Turning to another controversial issue, the profession remains divided at both the national and state levels on the matter of the training, employment, and statutory credentialing of master's degree clinicians. More than 200 APA-approved (as opposed to accredited) terminal master's programs train approximately 8000 graduates each year, nearly twice the number of doctoral graduates (APA, 1990b). Despite many recommendations to accredit master's programs, APA still reserves its accreditation procedure for doctoral level training (an exception is accredited master's school psychology programs). Furthermore, though it accords associate membership in APA to master's level psychologists, APA (1987a) has steadfastly ruled that a doctorate is the minimal requirement to be licensed as a psychologist. The uncertain status of the master's degree is also found in statutory credentialing at the state level, where only 13 states offer master's level licensure (as opposed to certification), and only 3 of the 13 states use the designation of master's level psychologist (APA, 1990b). In the other states, master's level psychologists must either practice under an alternative professional certification or license (e.g., social worker, counselor, mental health technician) or with exemption from state law (Dale, 1988).

The reality is that for economic reasons (e.g., lower salaries for master's level psychologists enhances their marketability) and manpower needs (e.g., shortage of Ph.D. psychologists in rural communities): universities continue to graduate master's psychologists; agencies and institutions continue to hire them (and for the most part are satisfied with their performance); and state licensing boards continue to vacillate between disenfranchising them or "making honest psychologists of them." In the meantime, master's level psychologists who can qualify academically may escape from their professional cul de sac by matriculating at one of the university-based programs or freestanding schools for doctoral training.

On an upbeat note, the council of Applied Master's Programs in Psychology (CAMPP), which was officially launched in 1988, has adopted a strong advocacy role to protect current and upgrade future professional status of master's level clinicians who, according to Stapp, Tucker, and VandenBos (1985), make up 35 percent of the psychological personnel in mental health services. On that basis alone, a realistic prediction is for subdoctoral education to continue into the twenty-first century.

An emerging trend in the 1980s, which has gained even greater visibility in the early 1990s, is the changing perception of postdoctoral training; that is, from an initial career step for a limited segment of doctoral graduates to an initial career pathway for all doctoral graduates, particularly those who expect to be primarily practitioners. A very likely outcome is that postdoctoral education will become an extension of predoctoral education—if not required, at least strongly encouraged.

There are at least three reasons for the changed perception. Let us consider them in the order of least to most pragmatic. First, an increasing number of state licensing boards require one to two years of supervised practice beyond the doctorate to qualify for full licensure. Second, of the expanding number of specializations and subspecializations, only a few can be acquired during predoctoral study and internship training; the evolution of clinical psychology from a mental health core specialty to a full fledged health care specialty has led to an ever-widening scope of clinical practice that far exceeds the generic professional psychology doctorate. Third, it is anticipated that part of the requirement for becoming an "approved" provider of psychological services in the nation's managed health care system will be evidence of certified proficiency in the diagnosis and treatment of specific disorders. In response to the above and other considerations, there has been a proliferation of postdoctoral training programs. And to address issues such as models of postdoctoral education and training, criteria for performance evaluation, and accreditation standards, two national conferences have been held, the first in 1992 and the second in 1994. There has been a controversial decision by APA to establish a National College of Professional Psychology to coordinate continuing education, postdoctoral training, and certification of advanced proficiency in designated practice areas (APA, 1994d). Although the recommendation was first made to APA in 1981, it took another 10 to 12 years to implement the recommendation to the point of obtaining APA's imprimatur. What the development will mean for organizations such as the American Board of Professional Psychology (which is psychology's oldest and most highly esteemed credentialing body), APA's Education and Training Board, the APA Committee on Accreditation of Professional Training Programs, and the Association of State and Provincial Boards of Psychology, is not yet clear. However, to many experimental and nonclinical applied psychologists, it is likely to be perceived as further evidence of APA becoming an organization for practitioners and one controlled by them.

RELATIONS WITH OTHER PROFESSIONS

Clinical psychology has always had and probably always will have uncertain (some would say stormy) relations with other health care professions. Cummings and VandenBos (1983) state: "The phrase, relations with other professions, most often translates into relations with Psychiatry" (p. 1324). Several professional developments that began in the 1970s and came to fruition in the 1980s, for instance, admission of psychologists to psychoanalytic training institutes, to hospital staff membership, eligibility for insurance by third-party payers, have further strained the uneasy truce between clinical psychology and psychiatry. The moderate voices in both professions have sought to soften the conflict points and to turn acrimonious debates into "good faith" negotiations. However, as clinical psychology encroaches further on psychiatry's domain of practice, economic competition will intensify. Some of the "pressure points" include: expanded hospital practice privileges for psychologists; recognition of psychologists as independent Medicare providers; an enlarged scope of practice for psychologists that may eventually include limited prescription privilege; and aggressive advocacy for inclusion of psychologists as autonomous providers in all federal and state health care programs. In fact, one could interpret psychiatry's increasing medicalization of mental health as a response to economic competition from clinical psychology; witness the latest revision of the *Diagnostic and Statistical Manual of Mental Disorders* (DSM-IV) (American Psychiatric Association, 1994), the noticeable shift of treatment time from psychotherapeutic practice to medication management practice, and the growing hegemony of a biological orientation in psychiatric residency training. Both professions might well heed Stanley Graham's (1989) down-to-earth caveat: "What must be done to survive? First, we must stop biting each other on the rear end" (p. 10).

On a more upbeat note, clinical psychology's relations with other nonmedical health care professionals, such as social workers, psychiatric nurses, and dentists, have been characterized by a spirit of collaboration and at the levels of both clinical practice and research projects. And one official step toward interprofessional cooperation is the Joint Commission on Interprofessional Affairs (Cummings and VandenBos, 1983) which has been approved by each of the four core mental health professions of psychiatric nursing, psychiatry, psychology, and social work.

RELATIONS WITHIN PSYCHOLOGY

Shortly after its inception as a formal discipline in 1892, relations between the experimental and applied branches of psychology began to alternate between periods of schisms and adversarial relations, and periods of detente and mutual respect. As noted earlier, an irreconcilable rift over academic versus applied interests and representation in APA led clinicians to leave APA in 1917 and to form their own separatist organization; of course, within two years the clinicians returned to the APA fold. Twenty years later the scenario was repeated, except that this time it took eight years of fence mending before the maverick clinicians returned to APA.

Perhaps prophetically, Albee (1970) surmised that "basic incompatibilities between the science of psychology and the profession of psychology may be so serious as soon to require [another] separation or divorce" (p. 1078; quoted in B. N. Phillips, 1989, p. 3). In 1988, a reorganization plan that ironically was designed to bring the scientific–academic membership up to or at least close to parity with the professional–clinical membership failed to muster the necessary votes (APA, 1988). This time it was the experimental (and many nonclinical applied) psychologists who left. Shortly thereafter, the splinter group formed an alternative organization, the American Psychological Society, along with its affiliate for clinical researchers, Association for Advancement of Applied and Preventive Psychology (AAAPP).

By the mid-1990s there are still no signs of rapprochement, even though APA has taken steps to give better representation to its scientific and nonclinical members by establishing directorates for science, education, and public interest, following the creation of the practice directorate. In the meantime the professional and other costs of the split are increasing. For instance, it is more costly to maintain two national organizations; psychology can no longer speak with a single unified voice on critical matters, such as federal funds for training and education, health care reform, and various sociopolitical phenomena that affect large segments of society. There is also the weakening of the integration of science and practice that has given clinical psychology its distinctive character vis-à-vis the other mental health professions.

To underscore the necessary interdependence of both traditions in psychology, Raymond Fowler (1990) aptly concluded in his APA presidential address: "Rather than saying that science drives practice or that practice drives science, it would be more accurate to say that they are synergistic" (p. 5).

More recently, the clash of the two cultures of science and practice has also been manifested within the field of clinical psychology. To wit, one has only to witness the ongoing split between the two camps of scientist-practitioner and practice oriented clinicians over training philosophies, guild interests, and political advocacy. As several spokespersons have pointed out, it is shortsighted to minimize the differences and gloss over the incompatibilities between the two groups. Instead, it behooves the profession to acknowledge, understand, and one hopes, make the differences more complementary than conflictual. Conway (1988) surveyed clinical psychologists who were independently identified as exemplars of either clinical scientists, scientist-practitioners, or practice oriented clinicians. Although possessing the similarities one would expect of highly educated and trained persons from the same discipline, the three groups differed noticeably on epistemic beliefs and values, theoretical orientations, and several cognitive and interpersonal attributes. Moreover, they were differentially shaped by their respective graduate educational experiences: "In short, they do what they do— be it research, clinical practice, or both—because of who they are" (Conway, 1988, p. 653).

Interestingly, many of the practice oriented clinicians were both interested and to some degree involved in research activities, a finding reported shortly thereafter by Norcross et al. (1989b): "Psychological practitioners who both consume and publish research appear to be the rule rather than the exception" (p. 51). To return to Albee's (1970) statement quoted above, he then goes on to say that "finding the roles of scientist and professional incompatible when existing within the same individual does not mean that scientists and professionals do not need each other" (p. 1080; quoted in B. N. Phillips, 1989, p. 4).

LAW, LEGISLATION, AND STANDARDS

The 1980s have witnessed the struggle of the profession to protect its accomplishments and, at the same time, to overcome the barriers that have excluded or threaten to exclude its participation in a wider sector of the health care delivery system. By far the major offensive thrust of the profession has been directed toward the practice of psychology in hospitals and other health care facilities, and inclusion in major third-party legislation.

To gain recognition as a primary health care provider without having to be authorized or supervised by a physician, the profession has centered its legislative agenda in three areas (Julius and Handal, 1980). The first is to improve regulation and control of the definition of psychologist through licensing and certification statutes. The profession has steadily progressed in this respect; the majority of states now define practice over and above the definition and limitations of the title psychologists (Stigall, 1981); and between the mid-1970s and mid-1980s, the number of licensed psychologists rose from 20,000 to 46,000 (L. Sechrest, 1992). The second agenda item is to obtain an amendment to include psychology for third-party reimbursement programs at the federal level. The third part of the agenda is to facilitate the public's increased access to nonmedical mental health providers via freedom-of-choice legislation in each state.

The second and third efforts yielded impressive results during the 1980s and into the early 1990s. There was a precedent-setting change in the Federal Rules of

Criminal Procedure that gives psychologists complete parity with psychiatrists through all parts of the Criminal Code (APA, 1985). This legislative change permitted psychologists to examine, treat, and testify in court under provisions relating to the federal criminal court system. Another successful effort has been directed toward the Deficit Reduction Act of 1985, which includes an amendment to allow psychologists to deliver services in risksharing health maintenance organizations (HMOs) without physician supervision and referral that is otherwise required for Medicare-covered services (APA, 1985). The amendment also was the first direct mention of psychology in the Medicare statutes.

There are two other examples of achieving parity with psychiatry that merit attention. First, the successful settlement between 1987 and 1991 of a lawsuit against the American PsychoanalyticAssociation removed the exclusion of psychologists from psychoanalytic training institutes and from membership in the American PsychoanalyticAssociation. Second, the new federal regulations by the Health Care Financing Administration now permit psychologists to assess both prospective and current nursing home residents for mental illness and retardation (APA, 1993f).

There are various other governmental recognitions and authorizations being accorded to clinical psychologists. Since 1987, the profession has been authorized by law to determine mental health disability in Social Security Administration programs (Novack, 1987). So far, 25 of the 50 states and Washington, DC, recognize psychologists as reimbursable providers in Medicaid, though there is much variability from state to state in covered services and methods of reimbursement (Resnick, 1983). Furthermore, signal legal and legislative victories have been achieved (e.g., in Virginia) in terms of Blue Shield reimbursement of psychologists for delivery of mental health services, and in modifying the exclusionary policy of the Joint Commission on Accreditation of Hospitals (JCAH) for the practice of psychology in hospitals and other health care facilities (Zaro, Batchelor, Ginsberg, and Pallak, 1982).

As for workers' compensation programs, legal authorization for clinical psychologists has been slow to develop. With the exception of Florida, Hawaii, and the federal system, psychology was not, as of 1987, formally recognized in workers' compensation laws in the other states, though unofficially psychologists are usually allowed to diagnose and treat (Merrikin, Overcast, and Sales, 1987). Since the foregoing survey, however, marked advances have been made toward including clinical psychologists in workers' compensation programs, and it is only a matter of time, it would appear, until full acceptance is awarded to clinical psychologists.

In taking its case to legislatures, courts, and regulatory bodies, the profession has argued that inclusion of psychologists as independent, reimbursed providers in the nation's health care system will not increase the cost burden of the system; in fact, it will quite likely reduce the demand for medical care and hospitalization. Wiggins' (1984) conclusion remains as timely as ever: "Now the struggle must continue on a state by state, hospital by hospital basis, with the one central issue remaining patient need and the qualifications, credentials, training and experience of the individual psychological practitioner" (p. 50).

Perhaps the single most important, certainly the lengthiest, legislative accomplishment has been securing recognition of psychologists as independent providers for Medicare authorized to receive direct reimbursement for diagnostic and therapeutic services under Medicare Part B, effective July 1, 1990 (Advance Plan, 1990; APA, 1990a). DeLeon (1986) reports: "Medicare is the major federal health care initiative . . . accounts for approximately 80 to 90 percent of all federal health care expenditures . . . [and] is the basis for federal health care policy" (p. 5).

Consequently, the profession stands to gain from this legislative landmark for many years to come; and, as has been true of so many legislative landmarks, many will benefit from the vision and perseverance of a small number of psychologist advocates. For example, psychologists' involvement in state Medicaid programs will likely be speeded up; and as those close to the action point out, hospitals often consult Medicare regulations to rule on staff membership and clinical privileges. So far, however, in only about half of the states have psychologists been approved for reimbursement as independent health care providers for Medicaid recipients. More significant, however, is that with inclusion in Medicare, psychologists have now secured an independent provider status in nearly all federally funded health care programs. Again, it seems likely that it will only be a matter of time before clinical psychologists have unfettered or unreserved acceptance in, particularly, federally sponsored health care benefits programs.

Flush with success and perhaps mindful of the ancient Roman principle, carpe diem, the profession has mobilized its resources to overcome two remaining, albeit redoubtable, barriers to full and collaborative participation in the nation's health service delivery system. The first is inpatient hospital practice, and the second is prescription privileges. With respect to the first barrier, Enright, Resnick, Ludwigsen, and DeLeon (1993) cite three significant developments that have set the stage for what the profession hopes to achieve in the 1990s. The first was the growing presence in the 1980s of for-profit psychiatric hospitals that for economic, and perhaps other reasons, have given psychologists direct access to inpatients. Moreover, direct access to inpatients, albeit to a much more limited extent, has occurred in public psychiatric hospitals as well as nonpsychiatric hospitals. The second significant event was the 1985 decision by the Joint Commission of Accreditation of Hospitals (JCAH) to broaden its authorized designation of medical/dental staff membership to include nonmedical practitioners. In 1991, the new hospital accreditation body, the Joint Commission on Accreditation of Health Care Organizations (JCAHO) specifically recognized licensed nonphysician professionals who are now permitted by state law and by the hospital to provide direct patient care without supervision by another discipline, as long as they are practicing within the scope of their licensure and in accordance with the privileges granted: "this policy change has truly opened the door for psychology's formal recognition within the hospital environment as a bona fide health care profession" (Enright, Resnick, Ludwigsen, and DeLeon, 1993, p. 137). The third and most highly publicized development was the 1990 California Supreme Court decision (CAPP v. Rank) that upheld the California psychologist hospital practice statute that gave psychologists the authority to admit, diagnose, and treat independently. Although similar hospital privileges were already in place in several other states, the California court decision was considered a pivotal one due to the state's large population and the vigorous opposition mounted by the medical profession. Shortly thereafter, a survey of nearly 600 hospital-affiliated psychologists by Litwin, Boswell, and Kraft (1991) revealed that most of the respondents could do in-hospital testing, research, and psychotherapy independently, but only a small percentage could admit, order medical referrals, and discharge without supervision. Thus, in many states psychologists have only limited medical staff membership and only ancillary clinical privileging, with little or no participation in hospital governance. As of the early 1990s, 23 states and Washington, DC, had enacted laws to implement the revised JCAHO policy on nonphysician providers in hospitals; 9 states and Washington, DC, had legislated specific hospital practice laws; and 12 more states have introduced legislation (Ludwigsen and Albright, 1994).

There is no question that attempts to overcome the first barrier of inpatient hospital practice have further strained psychology's relations with psychiatry. However, mounting a challenge to the second barrier, that of seeking legal prescription-writing privileges, has galvanized opposition not only from the medical profession as a whole, but also from many nonclinical and clinical psychologists. Despite the opposition from within and outside psychology, the drumbeat has become louder (DeLeon, Fox, and Graham, 1991, refer to prescription privileges as "psychology's next frontier"). Many observers believe the seed was planted by the encouragement Senator Daniel K. Inouye gave to the idea in his 1984 keynote speech to the Hawaii Psychological Association (DeLeon, Fox, and Graham, 1991). The proposal was picked up and given increasing attention in journals and practice group newsletters during the late 1980s. In response to the perceived groundswell of interest, the opposition notwithstanding, APA's Council of Representatives established a task force to study the desirability and feasibility of pursuing prescription privileges for psychologists; a year or so later the task force published a summary of its recommendations that included a model curriculum (Smyer, Balster, Egli, Johnson, Kilbey, Leith, and Puente, 1993). Concurrently, and independent of APA's actions, Congress authorized the Department of Defense, beginning in 1991, to sponsor a demonstration program to train a few military psychologists to prescribe a limited set of psychotropic medications (DeLeon, Fox, and Graham, 1991).

Proponents for prescription training cite the following arguments. Without prescription privileges, psychological practitioners can never assume full responsibility for the mental health treatment of their clients-patients; underserved populations (e.g., the elderly, the indigent, and chronically mentally ill) and geographical areas (rural, inner city) would benefit were psychologists to obtain prescription-writing privileges. Several other nonphysician

practitioner groups have been trained to independently
prescribe a limited range of medications for health conditions for which they already have expertise to treat (e.g.,
dentists, optometrists, podiatrists); and in parts of the
federal system, psychologists have already been legally
prescribing (e.g., Indian Health Service, Department of
Veterans Affairs). On the other hand, opponents warn that
obtaining the right to prescribe medications will turn out
to be a pyrrhic victory insofar as it will weaken psychology's
distinctiveness and uniqueness within the health care
arena; that research and training in psychotherapy will
suffer; psychology and psychiatry will become irreversibly
polarized; and that the tangible and intangible costs of
incorporating prescription training into graduate education will be too great to accommodate. Both positions have
merit. Nevertheless, the graduation of the first two
psychologists from the Department of Defense sponsored
training program, two more enrolled in the program, and
five more accepted for admission (DeLeon, 1994), together
with a developing state-level grass roots movement to have
limited prescription privileges included in state licensing
law, certainly strengthens the hand of the proprescription
group.

POLITICAL ADVOCACY

For psychology to be perceived as a fully legitimate science and a bona fide health care profession, political reality dictates that effective communication evolve between
the psychological scientists and practitioners on the one
hand, and the policy makers of the nation's health care
and scientific research systems (DeLeon, VandenBos, and
Kraut, 1984).

Because psychologists represent only a small propor-
tion of health service providers and lack seniority within
the health care professions, they must adopt a proactive
rather than a reactive stance in order to increase their

visibility with policy makers (Dorken, 1981). There are two strategic considerations, the first of which is to convince policy-making bodies that what is good for psychology is good for society. An optimal balance must be maintained between professional guild interests and the interest of the public at large. The second consideration is to discover politically sensitive methods to increase credibility and influence. What the profession has learned is the importance of orchestrating a multilevel, multidimensional approach that includes the strategic deployment of attorney-lobbyists, formation of political action committees (PACs), utilization of independent practice associations (IPAs), organizing grassroots fund-raising support for lengthy legal and legislative battles, setting up data-based presentations for legislators and citizen advocacy groups, and developing a national and state organized network of financial and sociopolitical resources.

Shaping public policy is a critical effort for all clinical psychologists. Hosticka, Hibbard, and Sundberg (1983) describe an advocacy position for public policy in which psychologists actively support the goals and priorities that will benefit both the profession and well-being of citizens. Smith (1990) underscored the urgency of balancing the profession's self-interests with a commitment to public interest goals, such as (1) establishing a pro bono tradition; (2) investing resources in social action programs for society's disenfranchised minorities of the underserved, chronically mentally ill population, and the plight of the homeless and hungry, neglected and abused children; and (3) for addressing the serious environmental problems that pose a threat to the nation's health.

As various pundits of the profession have advised, it seems logical to forget the technical, high-powered presentations. Legislators appear to attend and respond better to human interest stories and easily remembered vignettes that illustrate what the science and profession of psychology can and is doing for the public interest. A case in point

is the Disaster Response Network of Psychologists established by APA and the Red Cross.

Hosticka, Hibbard, and Sundberg (1983) also urge
that the clinical psychologist serve as a technician consult-
ant to policy makers. This would involve the clinical psychologist learning how policy makers approach decisions
and how they translate information into action, and then
sharing with the policy makers knowledge of efficient and
effective methods to attain legislative goals (e.g., a national health care plan). DeLeon, Frohboese, and Meyers
(1984) conclude that many of the content areas in which
psychologists have expertise are relevant to a wide range
of congressional issues; moreover, the procedural skills
that psychologists develop during their scientific or practitioner training can help them to function effectively on
legislative staffs.

Kempler and Norman (1981) refer to a "political coming-
of-age" for psychologists in their appreciation of the importance of presenting a proactive and unified position
with an agenda that blends social responsibility, public
accountability, and enlightened self-interest. On a nuts-
and-bolts level, professional sources have suggested constructive actions to enhance the profession's visibility and
to strengthen its credibility on both state and federal levels. For instance, psychologists are encouraged to seek
careers in the public policy field (e.g., specific jobs, lobby-
ing, campaign specialists, political candidacy—note the
1992 election of Dr. Ted Strickland, the first psychologist
elected to the U. S. Congress). Obtaining jobs in the public policy field would not only compensate for the employment downturn in traditional jobs and give impetus to the
"new careers movement," but would also increase the
political clout of the profession. Mowbray, Miller, and
Schneider (1983) drew attention to the impact of the new
federalism of the 1980s in which states have a large and
more influential role in funding and policy development.
The authors encourage psychologists to seek jobs in state

mental health departments, again not only to offset the declining job market, but also to protect and bolster psychology's position at the grassroots level. On the other hand, Mowbray et al.'s position paper assumes a political climate favorable to public sector employment, which the November, 1994 elections have shown is no longer a safe assumption. Basically, the political strength that the profession has gained at the national level must be extended to the state level by collaborating with state mental health directors (many of whom are psychologists); helping state psychological associations to wield more influence; lending support to citizen advocacy groups, such as the National Alliance for the Mentally Ill; and conferring with other disciplines, such as nursing and social work, which have or have had similar agendas in order to counter Patrick DeLeon's well-intentioned complaint that "we spend too much time talking to ourselves."

Psychology's coming-of-age politically in the 1980s has not been without its downside. The failure of a proposal to reorganize the APA in order to redress the political imbalance that had developed between the scientific and professional constituencies led to the formation of a smaller, alternative organization, the American Psychological Society. However, still in place are APA's two professional oriented subsidiaries, the Defense Fund which assists with the cost of legislative battles, and the Association for the Advancement of Psychology (AAP), psychology's only national advocacy organization (which is now independent of APA). The AAP has added a political action component called Psychologists for Legislative Action Now (PLAN), which is funded entirely by donations from practitioners.

To lend further assistance to the goals of clinical psychology, in 1987 APA established the practice directorate to promote the practice of psychology on both state and federal levels through legislative and legal advocacy, education, and funding. Not to neglect its other (nonclinical) constituents, APA later established similar directorates to represent the needs and interests of the science, education, and public interest areas. Yet, many public policy sources and psychologists may wonder whether the schism within psychology which took place in 1988 has been bridged or whether it continues into the midnineties. Certainly it seems, probably to all concerned, that a lack of unity is too high a price to pay, especially since it thwarts advances in political and public policy advocacy.

Finally, APA has taken action to educate both the public and the profession. A National Policy Studies Unit has been formed to coordinate the gathering and disseminating of information to educate and lobby at the national and state levels. A national publication information committee has also been formed to develop, coordinate, and disseminate information about psychology's scientific and professional contributions. The *American Psychologist*, the official publication of the APA, has a public forum section in which legislators, regulatory agency officials, and politically informed psychologists educate the membership about relevant and imminent public policy developments. A statement by one of those politically informed psychologists, M. Brewster Smith, gives a needed balance to the thrust of this section and the previous one:

> On the professional side, I also believe that a strong and responsible profession of psychology is in the public interest. But continued warfare with psychiatry over issues of turf—essentially guild interests—may be to the disadvantage of the troubled people we claim to serve, who suffer from the heavy cutting of government funds that have supported both psychiatry and psychology. I think our reflex rejection of anything labeled as a "medical model" is self-serving and wrong. Many problems of "mental health" that properly concern us also have their medical aspects. And I do not like our recent single-minded focus on the financial aspects of practice—third party payments, health insurance, Medicare, and the rest [Smith, 1990, p. 535].

CONCLUSION

Approximately 100 years have passed since Lightner Witmer performed his midwifery role in the birth of clinical psychology, which a half-century later matured into the "Holy Trinity of postwar [World War II] clinical psychology" (Korchin, 1976, p. 45) with its unique blend of teaching, research, and practice. To honor the contributions of those clinical psychologists who have given the profession its rich heritage, APA's division of clinical psychology held a recognition ceremony for senior members of the division, aged 70 and older (Jones, 1989).

As part of this ceremony, a survey of 271 senior members was undertaken, and 161 members responded to the following three questions. First, what have been the most significant developments in the field that have impacted on your professional career? Second, what professional decisions have you made which had the greatest impact on your career and/or the career of others? And third, what has been the most fun, and/or the most satisfying, in your professional career? For the first question, the three most frequently cited developments were securing licensure, the developing roles and visibility of clinical psychologists, and progress in scientific knowledge. For the second question, the three most frequently mentioned decisions were to work in a university setting, to practice in a hospital or clinic, and to begin private practice. For the third question, the two most frequently remembered satisfactions were teaching, supervising, monitoring graduate students, and "seeing the results of therapy make a difference to someone." Despite an occasional critical comment or pessimistic statement, the survey responses were remarkably candid, upbeat, and forward looking.

In 1992, the science and profession of psychology celebrated its first centennial. In 1996, the profession of clinical psychology celebrated its first centennial in Philadelphia where Lightner Witmer established the first psychology clinic at the University of Pennsylvania. Indeed, there is much to celebrate, as well as to look forward to in the rapidly approaching twenty-first century. One can only hope that the current stewards of the profession will take steps to ensure that the profession does not become so professionalized, so institutionalized, so preoccupied with proprietary concerns, that it loses the capability to respond swiftly and flexibly to changing economic, social, and political priorities. And one might further hope that in the twenty-first century clinical psychology graduate students will study the profession's first hundred years, not only to know their roots, but also because "past is prologue."

Chapter 3

Becoming Trained I: Academic Preparation

It is realistic to be concerned about employment. The pursuit of training is expensive, requiring a huge investment of money and life itself in acquiring the credentials necessary to be a clinical psychologist. Thus, throughout this book, consideration is given to how to maximize career opportunities. Certainly a threshold issue for any profession, and clinical psychology is no exception, is being academically prepared. The cornerstone of employment in clinical psychology is to construct a set of academic credentials that are as honorable and distinguished as possible. Trying to take a short cut is ill advised; being willing to pay the price for high quality is the approach of choice.

The American Psychological Association (APA) is recognized by the U.S. Department of Education and the Council on Postsecondary Accreditation as the premier national accrediting association for specialties in psychology. Since the 1940s, APA has been accrediting doctoral programs in professional psychology (APA, 1986b, Appendix B, p. 1). Clinical psychology programs were the first to be accredited, followed by counseling psychology and school psychology, and later combined professional–scientific programs which meet the minimal criteria in two or more of the above three programs (APA, 1986b; Preface, p. ii). In addition, the APA accredits predoctoral internship programs that provide advanced training for the professional psychology doctoral programs.

The purpose of accreditation is "to promote excellence in doctoral education and training in those specialties of professional psychology designated, and thus to provide a service for the general public, prospective students, and the profession itself" (APA, 1986b, Preface, p. ii). It should be noted that the terms *professional psychology*, *professional psychologist*, and *professional practice* do not eliminate the traditional specialty training in clinical, counseling, and school psychology; instead, the terms affirm APA's position that in addition to specialty training, a trainee must acquire a generic core of basic and applied knowledge of psychology; hence, the captioned designation in the *Accreditation Handbook: Criteria for Accreditation of Doctoral Training Programs and Internships in Professional Psychology.* In essence, an accredited program means the following:

> The program is recognized and publicly labeled as a doctoral program in clinical, counseling, or school psychology (or appropriate combinations thereof). It is located in and supported by an institution of higher education that itself is accredited by one of six regional accrediting bodies also recognized by the Council on Postsecondary Accreditation. The program voluntarily applied for accreditation and, in so doing, engaged in extensive self-study of its program objectives, its educational and training practices, its resource support base, and its faculty, students, and graduates. The program also participated in a peer review of its operations by a site visit team of distinguished professional colleagues. The program was thoroughly evaluated by the APA Committee on Accreditation (comprising professional and public members) and judged to be in sufficient compliance with the APA Criteria for accreditation, to warrant accreditation status. These criteria include extent of institutional support, sensitivity to cultural and individual differences, training models and curricula, faculty, students, facilities, and practicum and internship training [APA, 1986b, Preface, p. 11].

Accreditation for both doctoral and predoctoral internship training programs is based on policies and criteria developed by APA's Education and Training Board and implemented by a committee on accreditation. These policies and criteria are revised periodically to reflect the changing and expanding field of professional psychology.

Accreditation has three levels: full (program meets all the accreditation criteria); provisional (program meets most of the criteria with the expectation of meeting all the criteria by the next evaluation date); probation (fully accredited program that is not currently in satisfactory compliance with the criteria) (APA, 1986b, Appendix A, p. 1). An updated list of accredited doctoral and predoctoral internship training programs is published annually in the December issue of the *American Psychologist* with a supplemental listing in the July issue.

Accredited programs must submit an annual report to demonstrate continued compliance with accreditation standards; fully accredited programs will have a reevaluation site visit every five years, provisionally accredited ones every three years, and programs on probation have one year to demonstrate compliance. As of 1993 there were 175 clinical psychology programs, 63 counseling programs, 43 school psychology programs, 5 combined professional–scientific psychology programs, and 430 internship programs with full or provisional accreditation (APA, 1993d). By 1994, APA-accredited doctoral programs numbered 177 in clinical psychology, 64 in counseling psychology, 43 in school psychology, and 5 in combined professional-scientific psychology (APA, 1994g); and in 1995, the list was supplemented with 7 more in clinical psychology, and 3 more in school psychology (APA, 1995).

A doctoral program may lack accreditation status because the program is too new, has failed to obtain accreditation, or the program faculty and institution administration have chosen not to seek accreditation. As an alternative to accreditation, some doctoral programs may seek recognition by the joint designation program of the American Association of State Psychology Boards and the National Register of Health Service Providers in Psychology (Ross, Holzman, Handal, and Gilner, 1991).

Accreditation, of course, does not guarantee employment or state licensure for graduates; yet, graduating from an accredited program will almost certainly improve one's prospects for employment and licensure. One widely cited study by Walfish and Sumprer (1984) examined job advertisements in the *APA Monitor* and found that 95 percent of the listed employers stated that they prefer to hire doctoral graduates from accredited programs. A further analysis by the authors indicated that nine times as many graduates of accredited programs obtained positions advertised in the *APA Monitor.* There is no evidence that preference for graduates of accredited programs has diminished since that time.

For a wealth of descriptive information on more than 600 graduate programs in professional psychology, professionals and prospective students should consult the book *Graduate Study in Psychology*, which is published by APA (see 1994f, with 1995 addendum) biyearly and in the intervening years republished with an addendum.

Until the late 1960s, the training of clinical psychologists was based on the Ph.D. scientist–practitioner model. Dissatisfaction with the model notwithstanding, the scientist–practitioner model has been repeatedly endorsed at each of the national conferences on graduate education and training from the 1949 Boulder Conference to the 1958 Miami Conference, the 1965 Chicago Conference on Professional Preparation of Clinical Psychologists, the 1973 Vail Conference on Levels and Patterns of Professional Training, the 1986 Mission Bay Conference on the Education and Training of Professional Psychologists, the 1987 Salt Lake City Conference on Graduate Education, and the 1990 Gainesville Conference on Scientist–Practitioner Education and Training for the Professional Practice of Psychology.

Beginning in the late 1960s, an alternative to the Ph.D. based scientist–practitioner training model, the Psy.D. (or occasionally the Ph.D.) practitioner model became a reality (see chapter 1). In the same year that the Vail Conference became the first major conference on education and training to officially endorse the practitioner model and the use of the Psy.D. degree; the University of Illinois Psy.D. program became the first to be accredited by APA (see chapter 1, 1970–1980). It is estimated that there are now approximately 40 programs that train Psy.D. professional psychologists (Ellis, 1992, p. 572), and more than 30 are accredited. Contrary to predictions in the previous decade, Psy.D. programs account for less than one-half of the graduating professional psychologists (Shapiro and Wiggins, 1994, p. 208), and the rapid growth rate in the 1970s and early 1980s has slowed noticeably (Ellis, 1992, p. 572).

Despite the continuing debate in the professional literature between advocates of the Ph.D. scientist–practitioner model and advocates of the Psy.D. (or occasionally the Ph.D.) practitioner model, it is evident that the latter has become a fait accompli. Indeed, all of the national conferences on education and training, beginning with the 1973 Vail Conference, have recognized the practitioner degree and training model, and since 1979 the accreditation's handbook employs the term *practice* or *practitioner model* when referring specifically to the alternative model.

Still unsettled is the issue of whether programs ought to be accredited according to the educational model espoused (as the traditionalists advocate). Nevertheless, whether one is pro scientist–practitioner model or pro practitioner model, a strong consensus exists for a generic core of basic psychology content and methodology, similar to that which the current APA accreditation guidelines call for. On the other hand, there is a lack of consensus over what courses and how many courses constitute adequate clinical or professional content. One small but encouraging sign of a detente between the rival training philosophies occurred at the 1990 National Conference on Scientist–Practitioner Education and Training insofar as the conferees were receptive to substituting the terms *professional* or *practitioner* for the traditional terms *clinical* and *clinician* (Belar and Perry, 1992).

Be that as it may, several conclusions drawn by D. R. Peterson (1985), architect of the University of Illinois' Psy.D. program in the late sixties, have held up, to wit: graduates of both programs perform about equally well; curricula of both programs are more alike than different; and the main difference between the two models is the attitudes and interests of faculty and students. Following are the main criteria on which both types of training programs are evaluated for accreditation.

INSTITUTIONAL SETTINGS

Accredited programs are found in four types of institutional settings. The largest number of programs are still housed in university psychology departments; the rest are located in autonomous schools of psychology within universities (e.g., Wright State University, Rutgers University); other educational or professional units within universities (e.g., medical schools, colleges of education or health); or freestanding schools of psychology (e.g., the California Schools of Professional Psychology).

The Accreditation Handbook strongly recommends that a freestanding school of psychology, of which there are currently about 20 (Peterson, 1991), become a part of, or at least have an affiliation with, a university because of the breadth and depth of the available educational resources. It seems likely that it is just a matter of time before the recommendation becomes a requirement, although it is still officially opposed by proponents of the practitioner model. In any case, if not affiliated with a university, accreditation policy requires a freestanding school of psychology to be an incorporated, educationally accredited, nonprofit institution with a board of knowledgeable and responsible trustees without financial interests in the institution's operation (APA, 1986b, Appendix B, p. 3).

Further, *The Accreditation Handbook* states that training programs must: (1) be clearly and publicly identified and labeled as a professional psychology program; (2) have an identifiable psychology faculty chaired by a senior faculty member who has clear authority and primary responsibility for all aspects of the program; (3) ensure a breadth of exposure to the field of psychology including practicum, internship, field, or laboratory research training; (4) be affiliated with an institution that provides reasonable financial support. Additionally, an appropriate institutional setting must have adequate facilities in relation to the educational mission of the institution and the program's training model and goals.

CULTURAL AND INDIVIDUAL DIFFERENCES

In faculty and student recruitment and evaluation, curriculum, and field training, training programs must demonstrate knowledge of and respect for cultural and individual differences. This criterion is further specified insofar as: "programs must develop knowledge and skills in their students relevant to human diversity such as people with handicapping conditions; of differing ages, genders, ethnic and local backgrounds, religions and life-styles; and from differing social and individual backgrounds" (APA, 1986b, Appendix B, p. 4).

As Mio and Morris (1990, p. 434) point out, the American Psychological Association has long recognized the importance of the above statement, dating back to the Vail Conference, and written into the 1979 accreditation manual and the 1981 ethical principles of psychologists; however, the rate of implementation has been uneven. Understandably, controversy about this criterion has developed because it does reflect what has been taking place in society at large. In fact, because of continuing misunderstanding about the intent and implementation of this criterion, the APA Committee on Accreditation has undertaken an examination of the rationale, meaning, scope, and implementation of the criterion (Committee on Accreditation, 1991, cited in Rickard and Clements, 1993).

TRAINING MODELS AND CURRICULA

As in other professions, classroom and field training have increased to accommodate the rapid expansion of knowledge and the necessity for greater breadth and depth of clinical skills. As a consequence, a professional psychology curriculum typically takes four to six years of full-time application to complete.

For the basic psychology component of the curriculum, accreditation policy requires education in ethical and legal standards of clinical research and practice, statistics and research design, and history and systems of psychology. Also, while not specifically mentioned in *The Accreditation Handbook*, computer literacy is essential.

Beyond the basic psychology component, trainees must demonstrate competence, either by passing a comprehensive examination or by successful completion of at least three course credits, in each of four content areas: biological bases of behavior (e.g., physiological psychology, psychopharmacology); cognitive–affective bases of behavior (e.g., learning, motivation, emotion); social–cultural bases of behavior (e.g., social psychology, systems theory); and individual behavior (e.g., abnormal psychology, developmental psychology).

It is imperative that curricula be flexible enough to allow for elective courses in related disciplines. Given the rapid development of computer technology, cognitive approaches in psychology, and mindful of the Congressional declaration of the 1990s as the decade of the brain, access to instruction in computer science, cognitive sciences, and neurosciences is especially timely. A leading psychology journal, *Behavior Therapy*, refers to the "Application of Behavioral and Cognitive Sciences" in its descriptive title.

For the professional skills component of the curriculum, accreditation policy requires that "every student become familiar with major assessment and intervention techniques and their theoretical bases" (APA, 1986b, Appendix B, p 7). This encompasses, but is not limited to, individual and group assessment methods, psychodiagnostic evaluation (including education in the use of *The Diagnostic and Statistical Manual of Psychiatric Disorders*, American Psychiatric Association, 1994), group and individual psychotherapy, behavioral therapy, consultation, and program evaluation.

The declining emphasis on assessment training and the increasing emphasis on intervention training noted during the 1970s and early 1980s (Kolbe, Shemberg, and Leventhal, 1985) has leveled off, which is most likely due to criticism of the adequacy of assessment training by graduates and internship directors and to state licensure requirements. Piotrowski and Zalewski (1993) surveyed 80 Ph.D. and Psy.D. clinical psychology programs and found that the emphasis in assessment and psychodiagnostic training was about the same as in the senior author's earlier study (Piotrowski and Keller, 1984). Intelligence testing still received the most emphasis in nearly all the programs. There was more emphasis on objective personality assessment than on projective personality assessment, although there has been a slight increase in emphasis on both methods over the previous decade. Requirements in assessment coursework were similar for both Ph.D. and Psy.D. programs. Overall, the respondents seemed to predict that the current emphasis on intelligence testing would remain constant; and a sizable percentage of the respondents predicted an increase in emphasis on objective personality assessment and behavioral assessment methods, along with a decrease in projective personality assessment. Attesting further to the current importance of assessment training, O'Sullivan and Quevillon's (1992) survey of 138 clinical psychology Ph.D. training directors, and 96 terminal M.A. training directors revealed that 100 percent of the doctoral programs and 97 percent of the master's programs trained students in psychodiagnostic testing.

As mentioned, training in individual and group psychotherapy and behavioral therapy has remained a staple in the professional psychology curriculum (see Kolbe et al., 1985). O'Donohue, Plaud, Mowatt, and Fearon (1989) surveyed 119 APA-approved clinical psychology doctoral programs all of which required at least one but typically two or three courses in therapeutic intervention procedures, with behavioral therapy and psychodynamic therapy the mainstays (at least in the late 1980s and to be joined in the 1990s by cognitive–behavioral therapy).

Strangely, training in group, marital, child, and family therapies (though increasing noticeably in the marketplace) continues to be given short shrift in the curriculum of many programs, particularly the more traditional ones. Not surprising, therefore, is the omission of any mention of these alternative therapies in the accreditation handbook. O'Donohue et al. (1989) found that less than 15 percent of the clinical psychology doctoral programs offer training in child, group, or family therapy. There are some indications that programs are attempting to compensate for the lack of therapy course offerings with training opportunities within specialized practica or internship consortia (this is true also for training in behavioral assessment and diagnostic testing).

In an effort to profile current clinical psychology training including similarities and differences between the scientist-practitioner and the practitioner models,

Steinpreis, Queen, and Tennen (1992) surveyed 112 (93 Ph.D., 18 Psy.D., and 1 Ed.D.) training directors in 88 universities, 15 university affiliated professional schools, and nine freestanding schools. On the average, nine course credit hours were required in assessment-diagnosis, 19 in psychotherapy/behavior change, and 15 in practicum. There were no significant differences between Ph.D. and Psy.D. programs in the number of required statistics and research design courses or required course credit hours spent in client contact, nor did the directors of the respective training models differ in suggested changes in the core curriculum. The main difference between directors of the two training models was the former's emphasis on developing a strong research component in the trainee's professional identity.

In a more recent profile of clinical psychology training, Mayne, Norcross, and Sayette (1994) surveyed 129 directors of APA-accredited Psy.D. programs, practice-oriented Ph.D. programs, equal-emphasis Ph.D. programs, and research oriented Ph.D. programs. Approximately 25 percent of the programs emphasize practice over research, another 35 percent emphasize research over practice, and the remaining 40 percent give equal emphasis. Close agreement was found among the four types of training programs on undergraduate preparation in statistics, experimental methods, abnormal psychology, biopsychology, and learning-cognition.

For most programs, the preferred minimum on each subtest of the *Graduate Record Exam* (GRE) was between 575 and 600; the preferred minimum for undergraduate Grade Point Average (GPA) was approximately 3.3.

Approximately half the programs subscribe to a cognitive–behavioral orientation with psychoanalytic, systems, behavioral, humanistic (in that order) receiving a much lower endorsement rate.

Psy.D. programs did accept nearly four times as many applicants as did the research-oriented clinical Ph.D. programs. However, 95 percent of accepted applicants in the latter programs received financial support compared to only 37 percent in the former programs.

Given available information, it appears that admission to APA-accredited clinical programs is not quite as difficult as it was in previous decades. There seems to be about a 10 percent acceptance rate now, as compared to a 3 to 5 percent acceptance rate in the past.

Consistent with accreditation policy on cultural and individual differences, a concerted effort has been in progress for some time to incorporate multicultural training (both didactic and experiential) in a professional curriculum. As of now, multicultural training targets four groups: Asian American/Pacific Islander; Black/African; Hispanic/Latino; and American Indian/Alaska Native.

Among the three specialty fields of professional psychology, counseling psychology has been the most proactive in implementing multicultural training in doctoral programs, dating back to 1982. Hills and Stozier (1992) surveyed 49 APA-approved counseling psychology programs and reported that 43 programs have at least one multicultural course, 29 have a multicultural course requirement, and 22 allow for subspecialty training in multicultural research practice. A decade earlier, Bernal and Padilla (1982) surveyed APA-approved clinical psychology programs and found that less than half offered minority-related courses, a situation that certainly has improved since then.

A watershed event has occurred in the state of Massachusetts' landmark decision (the first state to do so) to require of graduate students and those seeking psychology licensure, four hours of training in multicultural issues beginning in 1996, and at least one graduate course in race and ethnicity beginning in 1999 (*APA Monitor*, 1994e, p. 41). With other states expected to follow suit, multiculturalism will in the very near future have a strong presence in professional specialty training programs. Already an increasing number of textbooks on multiculturalism, and professional journals such as the *Journal of Multicultural Training and Development* and the *Journal of Cross-cultural Psychology*, have made their way into course reference lists and library holdings.

Not to be overlooked in the professional curriculum is an informed understanding of relevant APA policies on ethical standards, standards for providers of psychological services (especially guidelines for services to ethnic, linguistic, and culturally diverse populations), and standards for educational and psychological tests.

In addition to education in substantive content areas and development of clinical skills, the curriculum must include training in research that is relevant to the professional practice of psychology. *The Accreditation Handbook* (APA, 1986b) states: "The canons of science and scholarship rather than of any specific methodological paradigm should be the focus in research training and in the evaluation of the merits of research" (Appendix B, p. 7). This is a forward-looking statement, and as noted later, one that is only slowly, if at all, being implemented in professional training.

Being careful to sidestep controversy inherent in laying out specifics, *The Accreditation Handbook* includes as four acceptable categories of research projects: natural setting or laboratory research, action research, evaluation and follow-up studies, and demonstration projects. Several surveys support the implementation of a research component in clinical psychology training.

In O'Sullivan and Quevillon's (1992) survey of doctoral and master's programs, the majority of both degree programs require a master's thesis; close to 100 percent of the Ph.D. programs require a research-based dissertation; and a slight majority of doctoral programs require research work in addition to the thesis and dissertation.

Sayette and Mayne (1990) surveyed fully accredited clinical Ph.D. and Psy.D. programs. Predictably, they found that Ph.D. programs are slightly more likely to emphasize

research and Psy.D. programs are more likely to emphasize clinical practice. Interestingly, the survey revealed
that by far the most popular research topic is behavioral
medicine.

An issue nearly as argumentative as the amount of
required research training is the traditional versus nontraditional research methodology. Based on a survey of 62
directors of scientist–practitioner clinical training programs, Shemberg, Keeley, and Blum (1989) reported much
more support for traditional experimental or correlation
methodology than for alternative methodologies such as
surveys, library research, and case history studies. Round-
ing out the picture, Sanchez-Hucles and Cash's (1992) survey of 40 practitioner programs found that 90 percent
require a dissertation. Although only 25 percent mandated
that the dissertation be empirical, two-thirds of the completed dissertations used traditional experimental and cor-
relational designs, and the remainder utilized a variety
of nontraditional methodologies.

Setting aside the long-standing polemics in the literature about the amount and type of research instruction, enrichment of clinical psychology, including practice, is the
fundamental goal of research training. Meltzoff (1984) concludes that research training provides a respect for the
process of knowledge acquisition, a way of thinking about
issues, a readiness to evaluate the literature critically, and
a willingness to evaluate and modify clinical practice.

To safeguard the welfare of the public and to maintain
respect of the professional community, a training program
must have explicit policies and procedures for ongoing
evaluation of students' clinical competence. Since the mid-
1980s there has been a trend both to individualize trainee
evaluation and to establish performance-based evaluation
of clinical competence (Fantuzzo, 1984; Schacht, 1984).

Although *The Accreditation Handbook* stops short
of defining minimal competence for practice in terms of
performance-based standards, the expectation is that the

"practitioners" on the faculty are responsible for evaluating trainees' practice competence, which, as Binder (1993) and others have concluded, means the progressive acquisition of clinical skills with real clients and patients. In place of or in addition to performance-based evaluation of competence, programs typically employ ratings from practica and internship supervisors and from faculty who teach skill-based courses. There is also a presumption that programs based on a practitioner training model will have higher requirements for practice skills and scientist–practitioner programs will have higher standards for other types of professional competence.

As stated above, one objective of evaluating professional competence is to prepare trainees to meet state licensure requirements, the most stringent of which is the *Examination for the Professional Practice of Psychology* (EPPP). The EPPP is nationally administered with a cutoff score that varies from state to state.

Ross, Holzman, Handal, and Gilner (1991) analyzed the relationship between four psychology program characteristics and EPPP scores. With acknowledged limitations in the data set, they report that program means were significantly higher in clinical programs than in counseling and school programs, in Ph.D. than in Ed.D. programs (Psy.D. programs do not differ significantly from Ph.D. or Ed.D. programs), in programs located in a psychology department instead of an educational department or freestanding psychology school, and in fully or provisionally accredited programs than in probationary and nonaccredited programs.

Whether evaluation is directed toward basic or applied components of the curriculum, a policy on trainee rights and due process procedure must be in place. Standard guidelines refer to an adequate written program description, provision for periodic evaluation of and feedback to trainees, written prescriptions for remediating deficiencies, and a formal due process statement that ensures trainee input (Meyer, 1980; Miller and Rickard, 1983).

FACULTY

Accreditation standards underscore the relationship between quality faculty (within and outside the professional program) and sound graduate/professional training. *The Accreditation Handbook* states: "Faculty should be composed of experienced, productive persons who have a major time and career commitment to the program and who are identified with the program so that they can provide effective leadership modeling, supervision, and instruction" (APA, 1986b, Appendix B, p. 11).

Beyond the normal duties of teaching, research, and supervision, faculty members are expected to be active as licensed practitioners and committed to participation in continuing education. In order to provide trainees with advanced knowledge about special practice settings and clinical subspecialties, practitioners from the local community are recruited to serve as adjunct faculty.

The faculty must be large enough to offer the necessary advisement, teaching, and supervision of trainees' practice and research; yet it must be small enough to provide the requisite mentoring and modeling which are indispensable for developing clinical, scholarly, and research competence, as well as fostering a commitment to the program's training model and identification with the profession.

A program's training model is usually reflective of faculty theoretical orientations. Today the scientist–practitioner model is more often associated with behavioral and cognitive behavioral orientations, while the practitioner model tends to be associated with psychodynamic and humanistic orientations.

Two current survey studies differ in characterizing the theoretical orientations of APA accredited Ph.D. and Psy.D. programs. Piotrowski and Zalewski (1993) report that of 80 programs surveyed, 57 percent were eclectic, 13 percent behavioral, 8 percent cognitive behavioral, 7 percent psychodynamic, and 15 percent other. Slightly different results from 115 programs were obtained by Sayette and Mayne (1990) with 42 percent cognitive behavioral, 26 percent psychodynamic, 14 percent behavioral, and 18 percent other.

The Accreditation Handbook specifically mentions that faculty should model the professional and interpersonal skills that trainees are expected to acquire, and also demonstrate for trainees how to integrate theory, research, and practice. Some faculty members find this challenge too problematic, that is, they cannot model or accomplish what is expected of their students. Consequently, accreditation site teams are somewhat lenient in their evaluation of this issue.

The problems associated with modeling specific clinical skills and effective integration of teaching, practice, and research have been sources of recurring criticism of scientist–practitioner training programs (see Peterson, 1985; Clement, 1988; Baum and Gray, 1992). An excerpt from Clement's (1988) recommendations serves as a clarion call to training faculty:

> In general, each faculty member should integrate his or her research, professional practice, teaching, training, and supervision so that each area of responsibility complements and builds upon the other . . . professors of professional programs should on a regular basis model the professional skills and procedures that they practice and teach. This modeling should be done with real-world clients/patients as doctoral students watch [p. 254].

The onus, of course, must be shared by psychology departments and universities as a whole, namely for rewarding faculty far more for research and scholarly achievement than for comparable achievement in teaching and training. To motivate faculty to model clinical skills and accomplish effective integration of practice, teaching, and research, universities should give as much recognition to exemplary training as they do to research productivity and scholarly accomplishment. More to the point is Kalinkowitz's (1978) well-tempered statement that: "As academicians, we can acknowledge that the professional reputations of our practitioner colleagues represent the same measures of skills and proficiency as our own benchmarks of excellence in teaching and research, and we can help convince our deans and presidents that years of professional expertise merit consideration for professorships and tenure" (p. 5).

In the area of human dignity and personal rights, accreditation policy makes it clear that programs must only recruit and retain faculty who are respectful of and appropriately responsive to individual differences in lifestyle, age, handicapping conditions, gender, ethnic and racial background, and religion. Legislation, of course, issues numerous mandates in support of this policy, such as through the Americans with Disabilities Act.

Further, programs are expected to document efforts to recruit and retain a faculty group that reflects the diversity in the population. From a data-based point of reference, the Council of University Directors of Clinical Psychology (February 1994) made available the results of a survey (N = 70 clinical directors) for the period of 1987 to 1993. The survey shows that within a typical clinical faculty of nine members, 29 percent are women, 8 percent minorities, and 1 percent disabled; these figures closely parallel results of the psychology departments as a whole with 27 percent women, 6 percent minorities, and 1 percent disabled persons.

TRAINEES

Key factors evaluated by an accreditation team are "the intellectual and personal characteristics of students, how they are selected, the nature of their interaction with faculty, and the manner in which students are helped by faculty in achieving their goals" (APA, 1986b, Appendix B, p. 13). In addition to intellectual capability and personal suitability (e.g., self-awareness, interpersonal effectiveness, ethical sensitivity, respect for cultural and individual differences), trainees are expected to demonstrate a commitment to social justice and to improving the quality of life of those with whom they come in contact.

The Accreditation Handbook states that descriptive material furnished to applicants and trainees cover the program model and goals; the program's theoretical orientation;[1] types of professional activities trained for; available training resources and facilities; the various requirements to be met and how they are evaluated; practice, teaching, and research interests of faculty; typical size of the applicant pool and acceptance and attrition rates; age, gender, minority, and handicap composition of faculty and graduate students; opportunities for financial aid, academic and personal counseling.

Trainees are entitled to have specific advisement on grievance and due process procedures, periodic oral and written feedback on progress, and where indicated a remediation or termination plan. A sensitive issue comes up when a progress review indicates personal unsuitability for continuing professional training. Where the personal unsuitability lends itself to likely resolution by short-term counseling, a remediation plan would include a recommendation for counseling along with information on community facilities and practitioners. Personal unsuitability based on a serious ethical deficiency or legal problem might warrant a termination plan, provided due process procedures are followed.

---

[1]APA accreditation policy does not proscribe a strong emphasis on one theoretical orientation, so long as trainees are exposed to more than one orientation. An even-handed recommendation is for a program to adopt a middle-of-the-road position between the extremes of no theoretical orientation and only one orientation, inform a prospective student where a program is on that continuum, and if there is a dominant orientation, be sure trainees are well grounded in that orientation (Forehand, 1985).

Notwithstanding decisions by the program, the student does, of course, retain his or her legal rights. If a student is discharged from a training program, he or she could, potentially, go through the university's appeals route and on to a court of law in search of a judgment counter to what was imposed at the program level.

Like faculty, cultural and individual diversity of trainees is to be sought in the selection process: "Students of academic excellence and professional promise will not be systematically excluded on the basis of race, ethnic origin, sex, age, religion, or physical handicap" (APA, 1986b, Appendix B, p. 14). In terms of diversity representation, the survey by the Council of University Directors of Clinical Psychology (February 1994) revealed that within an average new enrollment of eight to nine clinical students, 15 percent are minorities and slightly less than 1 percent are disabled students; within a yearly average graduation rate of 5 Ph.D./Psy.D. graduates, 10 percent are minorities and slightly less than 1 percent are disabled students; average annual rates for premature attrition were less than 1 percent for all clinical students, minority students, and disabled students. In a much larger survey, the enrollment figure for minorities in doctoral clinical and other health provider subfields was slightly over 10 percent with virtually no difference between Ph.D. and Psy.D. programs (reported in Hammond and Yung, 1993). As an aside, in response to the federal Americans with Disabilities Act, accreditation teams are taking special note of the presence of faculty and students with physical disabilities, provision of facilities for the disabled, and availability of resources for problem resolution. Within clinical psychology, women continue to be well represented insofar as they comprise close to 60 percent of those accepted and graduated, compared to about one-third in the mid-seventies.

Application for admission to training programs is a complex, labor-intensive, and financially expensive process for students. Faculty members also find the admission procedures to be demanding and frustrating. In talking to the senior author (RHW), one clinical training director pointed at a pile of applications, saying, "Bob, I have about 700 applicants here, with about 75 percent appearing perfect on paper, and we're going to select about 12 to 15 of them—how can I make any recommendations that are based on objective data?"

Admission procedures have a twofold purpose: first, to identify applicants who demonstrate academic aptitude and performance, as well as personal suitability to be trained as a clinical psychologist; and second, to select from an acceptable pool those students who best match the characteristics of a particular training program.

Academic criteria, such as GPA and GRE scores, serve as an initial screening for admission. After this selection, it is common to consider nonobjective criteria, such as letters of recommendation, autobiographical material, awards and honors, and job and/or research experience (any publications early in the applicant's career would likely be heavily weighted). If there is a passing of muster, the applicant may receive a telephone or face to face interview; this opportunity is granted to roughly 5 to 15 percent of the acceptable pool. Based on one survey of 112 clinical psychology programs, 90 percent use the GRE to screen applicants and nearly two-thirds require an interview (Steinpreis et al., 1992).

For a typical clinical psychology training program, most of the applicants accepted turn out to be satisfactory trainees. A troubling issue, however, is that some of those not accepted would in all likelihood have been satisfactory if accepted, and might even have been, in some instances, superior to those who were admitted. In other words, there is nothing foolproof about the admission procedures, and many who are denied admission can justly find solace in knowing that the negative outcome reflected the faults of the procedural system and not personal or academic inadequacies on their parts.

As has been true over the years, gaining admission to a clinical psychology program is almost always more competitive than gaining admission to other training programs for other psychological specialties. For that matter, the admission standards for clinical psychology, some would argue, are often more exacting than the admission standards applied in other mental health disciplines.

Psychology programs tend to rely greatly on the GRE. As pointed out in the literature, predictive validity of the GRE suffers from range restriction. In one study (Dollinger, 1989) of 105 students over a 10-year period, range restriction was offset by discounting GRE scores because of cultural disadvantage and admitting qualified minority applicants. GRE scores, especially the Advanced Psychology Test, significantly predicted two criteria: number of failed comprehensive examinations and a composite index of progress through the program. Undergraduate GPA did not correlate significantly with failed examinations and only slightly with the composite index. Tryon and Tryon (1986) reported a surprising finding that GRE Verbal score is a promising predictor of trainees' client engagement skills.

In one of the few published studies (Berman, 1979) that related both academic (GRE and GPA) and nonacademic predictors (age, sex, ratings of autobiographical statements, letters of recommendation, interview ratings) to varied criteria (ratings of diagnostic and therapeutic competence, graduate GPA, and comprehensive examination scores), the findings were somewhat unexpected. Both academic and nonacademic predictors were related to diagnostic competence, but only graduate academic data correlated significantly with ratings of therapeutic competence. Overall, nonacademic variables added little to the predictive process.

Other authors have expressed skepticism about nonacademic variables such as letters of recommendation and interview ratings. Range, Menyhert, Walsh, Hardin, Ellis, and Craddick (1991) cite several weaknesses of letters of recommendation, such as redundancy, lack of standardization, and omission of applicant's limitations and areas to strengthen. Given the legal consequences of saying something negative about an applicant, it is understandable why an undergraduate professor, for example, might hesitate to be unfettered in writing a letter on behalf of an applicant.

After reviewing studies on the effectiveness of personal interviews, Rickard and Clements (1986) conducted a study, finding that accepted applicants who were interviewed by clinical faculty and advanced clinical trainees did not differ from accepted but noninterviewed applicants in faculty ratings of suitability for internship, clinical employment, and academic positions. On the other hand, Gluck, Babick, and Price (1979) found that the addition of a group interview for applicants initially screened on academic criteria produced a more cohesive group of entering students and a lower program attrition rate.

Traditionally, faculty have been reluctant to use peer evaluations as predictors except in a limited manner at the stage of personal interviews. This could be chalked up to a power or control issue on the part of some faculty; that is, they wish to believe that they, not others, best know the selection bases and are the determiners of important decisions. Regardless, one study found peer ratings to be one of the best predictors of successful completion of a professional psychology program, and one of the best (of the none too good) predictors of which trainees were likely to publish (Hirschberg and Itkin, 1978).

With respect to undergraduate preparation, a survey of directors of APA-approved programs indicated that undergraduate research experience garnered the strongest endorsement; next was a visit to the program; and then evidence of possessing computer skills (Eddy, Lloyd, and Lubin, 1987, cited in Walfish, Stenmark, Shealy, and Shealy, 1989).

Understandably, most studies have focused on admission from the standpoint of the program faculty. However, Walfish, Stenmark, et al. (1989) sought information on how applicants make their final decision from among clinical psychology programs to which they had been accepted. The authors report that the most important selection factors are the reputation of the program, the amount of clinical supervision provided, and the perceived emotional atmosphere of the program. Interesting, financial support, albeit an important consideration, was not among the most important considerations.

The American Psychological Association, through its Office of Program Consultation and Accreditation and the Education Directorate, has published a revised edition of the accreditation handbook. The new edition, effective January 1, 1996, though very similar to the 1986 edition, emphasizes further: cultural and individual differences and diversity; the commitment to public disclosure and constructive response to complaints against an accredited program; the necessity for periodic outcome evaluation of program effectiveness; and the importance of training students in empirically supported interventions.

Chapter 4

Becoming Trained II: Supervised Clinical Experiences and Critical Issues

Field training is an integral component of a professional psychology program. Trainees apply their clinical skills under close supervision in real settings with real clients with real problems. Field training starts with a series of supervised practica, integrated with formal coursework, in an on-campus or off-campus facility, and culminates in an internship experience off campus in a broad-spectrum facility.

Supervised clinical practice is typically a highly demanding situation, with emotions flowing. Kaslow and Rice (1985) refer to the internship experience as a transition period from professional adolescence to professional adulthood. The analogy would imply that practicum experience is the adolescent period. Indeed, both the practicum and internship can create considerable developmental stress and strain for trainees. It does seem as if issues of personal suitability for clinical work are more likely to surface in the practicum or internship period than in any other period during professional education.

To assure quality control, supervised clinical placements must meet certain standards. Both practicum settings and internship centers must maintain a close liaison with a graduate program, be reasonably compatible with the training model of the graduate program, and comply with APA standards and guidelines for providers of psychological services.

As prerequisite to and preparation for an internship, practicum training should begin early in the doctoral program, usually by the end of the first year, and consist of a minimum of 400 hours, of which at least 150 hours are direct client contact with a ratio of 1 hour of supervision for every 2 hours of direct service (APA, 1986b, Appendix B). In addition to diagnostic assessment, psychotherapy, research, and consultation, trainees participate in case conferences, prepare progress notes and treatment plans, and develop record keeping skills.

The practicum, for which trainees receive course credit and sometimes a stipend, may take place in an on-campus facility, an off-campus facility, or preferably a combination of the two. The advantage of an on-campus facility is that a training program can better maintain a balance between service, professional education, and research, while allowing clinical faculty to model the professional skills and attitudes which they teach in the professional part of the curriculum. The advantage of an off-campus practicum site is the presence of a more diverse client population with a wider range of psychosocial disorders. The advantage of both types of settings is that trainees begin to learn about real-world conflict of priorities and the inevitable compromises that emerge from the interplay of clinical, administrative, political, and financial interests.

In any case, a practicum site must be one that possesses high standards of service, a major commitment to training, and is compatible with the training objectives of the doctoral program. As a consequence, program faculty have traditionally been opposed to practicum training located in a private practice setting, notwithstanding the fact that full-time private practice has become a major career pathway. On the other hand, the advent of the alternative practitioner training model, and the development of large independent practice groups and associations that contract with managed care corporations, may lead to a more felicitous view of a private practice based practicum, albeit with more emphasis on the financial dimension (i.e., awareness that clinical psychology is part of the health care industry) than would occur at a university site.

The second stage of field training is the internship. To be approved, the internship must consist of one calendar year full-time or a two-year half-time paid appointment in one or more APA-approved internship centers. *The Accreditation Handbook* (1986b, Appendix B) defines the essential purpose of the internship experience:

> Internship should provide the trainee with the opportunity to take substantial responsibility for carrying out major professional functions (such as assessment/diagnosis, consultation, psychotherapy, research, report writing, and record keeping) in the context of appropriate supervisory support, professional role modeling, and awareness of administrative structures. The internship is taken after completion of relevant didactic and practicum work and precedes the granting of the doctoral degree [p. 18].

As with graduate programs, APA accredits internship centers and expects that APA-accredited internship centers will select students from APA-accredited professional programs. As of 1993, more than 400 internship facilities have been fully or provisionally accredited (APA, 1993c; an update of internships may be found in APA, 1994h and 1995).

Although the large majority of internship centers draw interns from graduate programs across the country, some centers accept all their interns from one graduate department or professional school. These centers are not separately accredited by APA, but are evaluated and approved in the context of the professional training program with which they are affiliated. Another option that provides a broader range of training experiences for interns is a group of geographically related, but administratively independent, facilities that pool their training resources to develop an internship which then seeks accreditation as a consortium. Understandably, with increasing complexity and size there are problematic management and logistical issues to be dealt with. Whatever the option, the internship facility must conform to all relevant APA standards and guidelines and maintain a collaborative relationship with a doctoral training program in order to facilitate the selection, advisement, and evaluation of interns.

Within the internship center, responsibility for training is generally vested in a senior-level clinical psychologist who has demonstrated superior professional competence and leadership. The professional psychology staff should be large enough to offer a variety of professional role models and should be licensed in the state in which they work, and those who are primarily responsible for clinical supervision should have completed an internship as part of their training. *The Accreditation Handbook* (APA, 1986b, Appendix B) sets forth detailed requirements of internship sites, among which are the following:

> Internship settings should develop and distribute descriptive materials in which the goals and content of the training program, including reference to the characteristics of the client population, are accurately and explicitly formulated, so that prospective interns and doctoral training programs may match the program emphasis with intern interest . . . intern recruitment procedures should protect the applicants' rights to make a free choice among internship offers . . . facilities such as office space, clerical support, research equipment, library resources, etc., must be adequate to the needs of the training program . . . opportunities for research and for professional contact with staff of other disciplines should be available . . . two hours per week for formally scheduled individual supervision is a minimum; more is desirable . . . interns should be kept informed of their progress in

the program by means of clearly identified evaluative sessions, with training and content designed to facilitate their change and growth ... the training program itself should evaluate its own effectiveness in achieving its goals with interns [pp. 22–23].

The book *Internship and Postdoctoral Programs in Professional Psychology*, published yearly by the Association of Psychology Postdoctoral and Internship Centers (APPIC, 1993–1994), is an indispensable resource for trainees planning an internship. The directory provides useful information about accreditation status (full, provisional, or nonaccredited but meeting APPIC membership criteria), number of staff and interns, stipends, distribution of training time, theoretical orientation, opportunities for subspecialty training, and types of doctoral programs from which the internship center will accept trainees.

Trainees must begin planning their internship well in advance of the February 10 date for notification of acceptance by an internship facility. This planning should usually start by the beginning of the third year of graduate study, and perhaps even earlier. Eggert, Laughlin, Hutzell, Stedman, Solway, and Carrington (1987) report that the market for interns continues to expand with an even stronger preference than in preceding decades for interns from APA-accredited programs, and APA-accredited sites attract many more applicants than do non-APA-accredited sites. Yet, more than half of the 350 interns in nonaccredited internships are from APA-accredited graduate training programs, and they cite location as their major reason for choosing a nonaccredited site (Solway, Huntley, Stedman, Laughlin, Belar, Flynn, and Carrington, 1987). The same authors note that finances are said to be the main reason for internship centers not seeking accreditation, and approximately two-thirds expect to seek accreditation eventually. Based on an analysis of APPIC data, Stedman (1989, cited in Tipton, Watkins, and Ritz, 1991) found that, in addition to a limited supply of males and minorities, there were 15 percent fewer trainees from APA-accredited programs than there were positions available at APA-accredited/ APPIC-member internship facilities.

Factors important in selecting an internship site are (in descending order): status, quality of supervision, geographical location, type of professional program, training and development emphasis, and staff's theoretical orientation (Krause and Lawlor, 1990). Often overlooked in the selection process are the approximately 8 to 10 APA-accredited military internships which offer the largest stipend, in addition to housing, education benefits, travel, and guaranteed postdoctoral appointment (Johnson and Wilson, 1993); as expected, the drawbacks are a three-year commitment, adaptation to a military culture, and a formidable application process.

Compared to graduate school application procedure, applying to and being accepted for an internship center is fraught with less anxiety and frustration but still with more than can be justified. Two procedures developed to ease the strain are early acceptance (Krause and Lawlor [1990] for a description and evaluation) and computer matching. Innovative procedures notwithstanding, selection factors accorded the most weight are still the conventional ones of amount and perceived quality of clinical practica, academic record, letters of recommendation, and personal interview (Petzel and Berndt, 1980; Sturgis, Verstegen, Randolph, and Garvin, 1980). As Ross and Altmaier (1989) point out, empirical support for the conventional criteria is lacking as is information on differential weighting of these criteria by different types of internship centers.

As has been true over the years, internship directors would like beginning interns to be more grounded in clinical coursework and supervised practicum experience (Shemberg and Leventhal, 1981). However, the traditional critical stance toward preintern preparation and toward

Psy.D. trainees has moderated somewhat (Snepp and Peterson, 1988).

For the record, the most important criteria in selecting intern applicants are still a trainee's informed understanding of the fundamental psychological processes in both normal development and developmental psychopathology, a modicum of proficiency in using *The Diagnostic and Statistical Manual of Mental Disorders* (American Psychiatric Association, 1994), coursework in psychodiagnostic assessment and to a lesser extent in psychotherapeutic interventions, and more supervised practicum than the 400 hours set forth by the APA accreditation standards (Shemberg and Leventhal, 1981; Tipton et al., 1991). Depending upon the particular internship center, other criteria have high priority such as cultural and individual diversity, perceived quality of the intern's training program, ratio of applications to openings, and a trainee's specialized interest and skills. Internship staff's evaluation of trainees at the end of the internship year are generally positive and upbeat about what has been accomplished (Tipton et al., 1991).

Although the controversy over generic versus specialization training persists (probably because it continues to be framed as either-or), many internship centers, like many graduate professional programs, offer both generic clinical training and, depending upon the expertise of the staff and client–patient population, subspecialty training or specific areas of concentration.

As has been true of professional psychology education in general since the late 1970s, there have been pockets of discontent and dissatisfaction both with the preparation of trainees for internship and with the internship experience proper. As in the case of other summit conferences on graduate psychology education, the angst found expression at the 1987 Gainesville National Conference on Internship Training in Psychology in a series of proposals and counterproposals to improve the quality of the internship experience (see Belar, Bieliauskas, Larsen, Mensh, Poey, and Roelke, 1989). Noteworthy is a proposal to increase the practicum prerequisite from 400 to 900 hours with most of the increase allocated to direct client contact and clinical supervision. Evident also is a seeming groundswell of support (at least among the conferees) to increase the internship from one to two years with the second year designated as postdoctoral, but as of now it is uncertain whether the second year will be designated as internship, residency, or some other term that is commensurate with an advanced level of training. As an aside, in the Steinpreis et al. (1992) study cited earlier, less than 20 percent of the 112 clinical psychology training directors favor increasing the internship to two years. Without endorsing the proposal of a two-year internship, the APA Committee on Accreditation has nevertheless gone on record in support of a proposal to complete the doctoral degree prior to internship (similar to medical education). To reflect the concern with professional standards for psychologists and credibility in the health care field, the conferees gave substantial support to a proposal that internship training only be conducted in APA-accredited sites, and that only trainees from APA-accredited training programs be accepted for internship.

Supervision is a critical link between didactic learning in coursework and experiential learning in clinical practica and internship; most supervision occurs in the field training portions of the curriculum (Woody and Robertson, 1988, p. 177). As defined by Schaefer (1981), supervision objectives are: (1) to assist a supervisee in developing a self-monitoring/self-evaluating mindset; (2) to train a supervisee for a future supervisory role; and (3) to teach therapeutic (and we would add psychodiagnostic assessment) skills, ethical responsibility, and skillful interpersonal behaviors.

The third objective is by far the most critical one. A supervisor bears a heavy responsibility to ensure supervisee's competence with designated clientele.

Relatedly, a supervisor may occasionally be called upon to address a supervisee's psychological impairment or dysfunction. Note that Lamb, Cochran, and Jackson (1991) provide guidelines for assessing and intervening in a supervisee's psychological impairment. Not only is a supervisor responsible for teaching ethical behaviors to supervisees, the supervisor must also demonstrate personal ethical responsibility by ensuring that he or she is qualified to supervise a particular supervisee, confidentiality limits between supervisor and supervisee have been clearly stated, and some effort is made to evaluate supervisory effectiveness (Newman, 1981, cited in Russell and Petrie, 1994).

Currently, the APA accreditation standard for practicum is one hour of supervision to two hours of direct service. In a survey of 150 predoctoral internships, Hess and Hess (1983) found a ratio of one hour supervision for every three hours of psychotherapy, with the APA accreditation standard being a minimum of two hours of one-to-one supervision per week.

Like any training method, supervision must be congruent with the skill and experience level of the supervisee. At the practicum level, the supervisory approach is primarily directive, structured, and clearly instructive in its thrust, so that a trainee can assimilate the fundamental clinical skills in a timely and efficient manner. During internship, this approach is characteristic of the early phases of the internship experience to be followed in the later phases by a more collaborative, consultative, mentor–mentee approach.

Supervision methods include: case presentation; audiotape or videotape presentation and analysis; direct observation of a session followed by supervisory input; and variations of "live" supervision. The latter can include direct observation through a one-way window, whereby the supervisor, while observing the trainee–client interactions, could talk by telephone to the trainee or enter a session and model the desired clinical and interpersonal skills for the trainee. Also, the supervisor and trainee can serve as cotherapists, thereby allowing modeling and subsequent supervision.

In a survey of 142 advanced clinical and counseling trainees, Allen, Szollos, and Williams (1986) found the best discriminators of supervision quality to be a supervisor's perceived expertness and trustworthiness in giving honest feedback, duration of the supervised training experience, and more supervisory emphasis on personal growth than on technical skills. High marks were given to supervisors who set forth specific expectations, gave clear feedback, and avoided sexist and authoritarian behaviors.

Moskowitz and Rupert (1983) surveyed over 150 clinical psychology trainees and reported that close to 40 percent experienced a major conflict in the interaction with their supervisor. Fortunately, in most instances the conflicts were discussed openly and resolved effectively, with conflicts over a supervisor's style being the least difficult to resolve and conflicts over a trainee's interpersonal style being the most difficult to overcome.

While a supervisory role is commonly achieved by virtue of experience, being a good supervisor requires more than experience alone. From a review of published research on supervision, Russell and Petrie (1994) found that beyond a very minimal level of supervisory experience, additional experience and having the terminal degree were not associated with trainees' self-report of greater supervisory competence and supervision effectiveness.

With respect to preparing a trainee for a later role as a supervisor, Hess and Hess (1983) found that close to one-third of the 150 internship centers surveyed offered some formal supervisory training. Unfortunately the prevailing sentiment still is that one learns to be a supervisor by being a supervisee.

Some doctoral programs do offer courses on supervision, usually in conjunction with consultation. Also, in a few practicum facilities, advanced trainees supervise beginning trainees with clinical faculty oversight (with emphasis on the advanced trainees' supervisory skills).

The bottom line seems to be that supervision training is a neglected part of the training of clinical psychologists. On a positive note, there appears to be a strong consensus that time should be made available in the curriculum of professional programs for both didactic and experiential training in supervision (Russell and Petrie, 1994).

SUBDOCTORAL TRAINING

After enjoying a steady increase for many years, the number of terminal master's clinical psychology programs and the rate of admission to the programs leveled off in the late eighties and early nineties. A most likely reason is the realistic fears and pessimism about the professional future of subdoctoral clinical psychologists. For example, state licensure requirements will only become more stringent, third-party reimbursement will only become more limited (i.e., cost-containment is not likely to be implemented by reimbursing master's level instead of doctoral level psychologists), and because of pressure for higher provider standards and credentials by the managed care sector, the domain of practice will only become more confined.

Traditionally, the master's degree has served three purposes: (1) as an intermediate stage in a doctoral program in which a trainee's progress can be reviewed and improvements made; (2) as an opportunity to train for clinical positions that do not require doctoral level skills (though preparation at this level ought to include minimally courses in diagnostic testing and behavioral assessment, individual and group psychotherapy, and a 500-hour supervised practicum); and (3) as a proving ground for bachelor's level graduates who are not accepted directly into a doctoral program.

Although some doctoral programs accept or transfer credits for courses taken in a terminal master's program, many do not. High profile doctoral programs may even be biased against accepting applicants who have completed a terminal master's program. On the other hand, Tucker and Annis (1981) support the purpose of being a proving ground, pointing out that the master's program provides more in-depth experience in professional psychology education than does the undergraduate curriculum; furthermore, a bachelor's degree combined with a master's degree (with thesis research) is a better predictor of success in doctoral study than the bachelor's degree alone.

Several studies report that master's level psychologists are often employed either full- or part-time while working on a doctoral degree; and also it is known that the majority are satisfied with their jobs and believe that their training adequately prepared them to do their jobs responsibly (Stevens, Yock, and Perlman, 1979; Erdwins and Buffardi, 1983). Surprisingly, psychotherapy is the most frequent professional activity for master's level psychologists, even though the emphasis in most master's programs is coursework on assessment-diagnosis.

A less optimistic finding is one by Havens, Colliver, Diamond, and Wesley (1982) in which directors of public mental health settings were surveyed on their perceptions of the professional capability of persons with Ph.D.s, master's, and M.S.W.'s. The master's degree psychologists were at the bottom of the professional hierarchy (e.g., in perceived competence, salaries, and promotion). Recommendations for training master's level psychologists surface regularly and range from support for the status quo, to collaborative training with another discipline (e.g., social work), to technician training programs separate from doctoral programs and with a job title other than psychologist. Note that the next chapter will deal further with issues pertaining to the employment of master's level psychologists.

RESPECIALIZATION, SPECIALIZATION, AND SUBSPECIALIZATION

Since the midseventies, an increasing number of psychologists with doctorates in nonprofessional fields have sought training in a practice specialty (e.g., a developmental or social psychologist who respecializes in clinical psychology). Subsequent chapters will discuss certain critical issues relevant to retraining or augmentation of nonclinical degrees.

Respecialization (which may also be called augmentation or something similar) is designed only for doctoral level psychologists. Ideally, respecialization should be in an APA-accredited program, and most certainly it should be from a properly accredited institution. Whatever the setting, respecialization should be according to an formalized plan, with organized and integrated training experiences.

Most commonly, respecialization training includes two years of coursework and practica, with an additional one-year (preferably APA-approved) internship. The Ph.D. degree must be solid enough to make a respecialization candidate eligible for state licensure, inasmuch as respecialization training provides only a certificate or nondegree diploma. The book *Graduate Study in Psychology* publication (APA, 1994f, with 1995 addendum) designates departments with a formal respecialization concentration, as well as departments that will take respecialization applicants into the regular predoctoral training program.

Although APA has recommended that professional psychology programs accommodate respecialization, the response from training programs has not been particularly encouraging. Stricker, Hull, and Woodring (1984) surveyed graduate psychology programs and found that 43 were involved in respecialization training and 26 of the 43 programs were in clinical psychology. Approximately 40 programs that accept respecialization applicants admit less than 5 per year (APA, 1983), and only 20 percent of APA-accredited programs accept respecialization applicants. Stricker (1983) reports that typically there are 15 to 20 applicants for four or five openings.

Specialty training typically refers to the professional specialties of clinical, counseling, and school psychology. Specialization and subspecialization refer to additional (i.e., beyond basic or generic) training in one or more practice domains of a specialty field. Opinion remains divided over the wisdom of specialization and subspecialization training at the predoctoral level, and to date accreditation policy has not included any provision or guidelines for specialization. The lack of provision is explicit in the APA (1989) Education and Training Board's Task Force Report on Scope and Criteria for Accreditation: "Accreditation of programs at the doctoral level are founded on a broad base of knowledge and methods in the scientific discipline of psychology, a 'professional core' of knowledge, skills, and attitudes, and an opportunity for students to apply these to the types of settings, populations, and problems represented in one or more fields of professional practice" (p. 17, cited in Beutler and Fisher, 1994). On the other hand, federal requirements that designate training grants for specific areas or for specific client populations provide a persuasive argument for the desirability of developing areas of concentration.

In the past, certain governmental sources gave financial support to training for special purposes. VandenBos and Stapp (1983) indicated that an increase in federal funds would train practitioners to work in rural settings, provide service to targeted populations (e.g., the elderly, minorities, handicapped), or concentrate on primary prevention and behavioral health. Rickard and Bernaty (1983) correctly point out that identification and selection of subspecialty offerings are influenced by perception of the need for the marketability of the specialized provider, and generic clinical training can add or drop subspecialty offerings as the need and availability of faculty resources and expertise change. Given shifts in public policies, priority for funding clinical training is currently unpredictable.

Current specialization or subspecialization within the professional specialty of clinical psychology include, but are not limited to: child clinical or pediatric psychology; correctional and police psychology; family psychology; school psychology; legal or forensic psychology; geropsychology; health psychology (encompassing behavioral medicine, public health, occupational health, rehabilitation psychology); multicultural/minority practice; clinical neuropsychology; public administration or management; rural psychology; and substance abuse and addiction.

CONTINUING PROFESSIONAL EDUCATION AND POSTDOCTORAL TRAINING

Related to the trend toward specialization and subspecialization is the responsibility of trainees to continue their professional education after graduation. The critical issue is whether Continuing Education (CE) is to be voluntary or mandatory, an issue that APA continues to waffle on.

Continuing Education garnered significant attention during the late 1970s in response to several concerns such as the observation that the "half-life" of professional knowledge may be closer to 5 to 6 than to 10 to 12 years (Kalafat and Neigher, 1983); increased demand for accountability by the public, government regulatory agencies, private third-party payers, legislatures, and consumer groups; and publication of survey reports critical of traditional training in clinical psychology. In 1979, APA's Council of Representatives addressed the issue by establishing the Sponsor Approval System to provide national standards for CE in psychology, a computerized CE registry, and a CE calendar clearinghouse (APA, 1984a).

Depending upon individual state guidelines, CE experience may be acquired by attending workshops and conferences, being supervised, formal coursework, publications, or presentations of papers (VandeCreek, Knapp, and Brace, 1990). By statute or rule, state licensing units may specify that CE credits for renewal of a license must be earned from a preapproved provider (i.e., a training facility that submits an application and its qualifications for review and approval by the state licensing board).

A noticeable trend over the past half-dozen years is for CE programs to be longer than the traditional one- to two-day workshop or conference. The purpose is to offer participants clear-cut skill training in addition to didactic knowledge. Participants earn certificates of proficiency instead of certificates of completion, which are more likely to strengthen job security, enhance prospects for job advancement, and fulfill requirements for third-party reimbursement.

In the context of the above, postdoctoral training is equivalent to the first step in CE for a newly minted doctoral level clinical psychologist. Postdoctoral training has become an extension of professional psychology training, and if not yet required, it is at least strongly recommended. As an employment aside, it is common today for the preferred applicants for jobs in clinical psychology, especially for university faculty positions, to have substantial postdoctoral training (not just postdoctoral work experience).

To accommodate this development, there has been a rapid growth in the number of postdoctoral training sites from 22 in the early 1960s to nearly 400 in 1993 with over 600 listed postdoctoral positions (Wiens, 1993). Attesting also to the significance of postdoctoral training is the title change of the Association of Psychology Internship Centers (APIC) to the Association of Psychology Postdoctoral and Internship Centers (APPIC), which now includes postdoctoral programs that have met criteria for APPIC membership (APPIC, 1993–1994). Relatedly, the current importance of and attention to postdoctoral training is underscored by the establishment of the first national conference on postdoctoral training in 1992 (Belar, Bieliauskas, Klepac, Larsen, Stigall, and Zimet, 1993) and the second held in early 1994 (APA, 1994e, p. 44). The next step would be to extend APA's accreditation procedures and standards to postdoctoral training.

Currently, postdoctoral training may be a one- to two-year period of supervised employment to fulfill a state licensure requirement, a one- to two-year clinical or research (or combination) fellowship, or a one-year extension of a predoctoral internship. In any case, postdoctoral training ought to make for a smoother, less difficult transition to a professional psychology career.

If moving out of the cocoon of a graduate training program into an internship is a stressful transition, making the transition to full-time professional employment may test one's mettle even more. The reason is that, unlike the internship, there is no informal preparation to help close the gap between idealistic or unrealistic expectations and real-world outcomes. Olson, Downing, Heppner, and Pinkney (1986) conclude that tasks such as learning to wear different professional "hats," understanding an organization's mission and politics, developing personal resources, and avoiding burnout are not ordinarily anticipated, much less addressed during training. Farber and Heifetz (1981) comment that career expectations of many trainees are unrealistically positive (e.g., high status and income, autonomy, personal fulfillment). The next chapter will deal with a wide variety of employment expectations and considerations, as relevant to the foregoing issue.

There was a recent (highly debated and contested) decision by APA to establish a college of professional psychology. If it accomplishes its objectives, the project bodes well for APA being able to acquire centralized coordination and control over rapidly developing changes in continuing education, postdoctoral training, and professional specialization (APA, 1994d).

The expectation is that the college will be modeled along the lines of existing accreditation procedures for doctoral programs and internships. Starting with the premise that a generic degree and license are insufficient in relation to the breadth and depth of psychology's domain of practice, the college will have probative functions of setting criteria for approved proficiency or specialization areas, guidelines for reviewing effectiveness of CE programs purporting to prepare practitioners for proficiency in specialized areas, and evaluation standards to certify competence in designated proficiency areas.

A pragmatic concern that gave impetus to the landmark decision is that psychological practitioners need (and will need even more in the future) certificates of specialization proficiency, with basically APA's imprimatur, in order to survive economically, much less succeed, in the stringently managed health care system. In short, the clinical psychologist of the future will need to be a more highly credentialed professional. Consequently, it is an understatement to say that receiving a doctorate will establish one's status as a clinical psychologist.

TRAINING EVALUATION

Over the past 20 years recurring criticisms about and recommendations to improve the adequacy and relevancy of clinical training have been made (Garfield and Kurtz, 1976; Norcross and Prochaska, 1982c; Kalafat and Neigher, 1983; T. J. Ball, 1985; Tyler and Clark, 1987). Suggestions for improvement include more coursework in assessment and psychotherapy, additional practica, and more closely supervised clinical experience by experienced clinicians. In general, nonacademic/research clinical psychologists who do not give high priority to academic and research notions are much less satisfied with the scientist–practitioner training and curriculum than are clinical psychologists who do give high priority to academic and research notions (Tyler and Clark, 1987). It appears that trainers have given consideration to the criticisms and recommendations. Over the past five to seven years, clinical training seems to have become more skill based, with more time allotted to practica (or other supervised clinical experience) and greater use of community practitioners as adjunct faculty members. Clinical psychologists appear to be pleased with the quality of their training. As a modest sign of continuing improvement, a survey of 579 APA members of the Division of Clinical Psychology by Norcross, Prochaska, and Gallagher (1989a) revealed that 68 percent were very satisfied with graduate training and 73 percent with internship training; 23 percent and 19 percent were either slightly satisfied or dissatisfied with graduate training and internship training respectively; and only 8 to 9 percent were very dissatisfied with graduate training and internship.

Nearly all the evaluation studies are based on retrospective judgments by former trainees whose time since degree completion varies widely. Much less evident in the literature have been reports of evaluation of training effectiveness conducted by training programs and internship centers. Although APA accreditation policy (APA, 1986b, Appendix B, p. 8) calls for an explicit comprehensive system of evaluation, the mandate is short on specifics. Accredited programs are expected to evaluate training effectiveness on matters pertaining to licensure regulation and other published standards for psychological practice; and thorough evaluation should be made of skill areas emphasized in a program's model of training (i.e., scientist-practitioner or practitioner). In Steinpreis et al.'s (1992) survey of 112 programs, the most common methods for maintaining standards and quality assurance were written evaluations of overall competency and achievements of trainees and faculty, trainees' evaluations of faculty teaching and supervision, and periodic external peer reviews.

Regrettably, published reviews of the evaluation of training effectiveness have been generally negative with only minimal improvement over time (J. D. Ford, 1979; Edelstein, 1985; Alberts and Edelstein, 1990). It may well be that too much reliance has been placed on retrospective impressionistic judgments by training faculty and graduates, anecdotal reports from supervisors and supervisees, quantitative measures of questionable reliability and validity, and failure to link ongoing evaluation to end-product evaluation (L. H. Levy, 1983; Alberts and Edelstein, 1990).

Norcross and Stevenson (1984) surveyed 62 directors of approved doctoral programs and concluded that informal, qualitative evaluation measures (e.g., personal impression, reputations) were used most frequently and formal quantitative measures (e.g., pre-postcomparisons) least frequently. Supervisors' written evaluations, APA-accreditation reports, verbal feedback from internship supervisors, and ratings of supervisors by supervisees had the most impact in judging the quality of clinical training. Only 2 percent of the programs employed a combination of faculty and trainees to do the evaluation. Stevenson and Norcross (1985) surveyed 131 psychology training clinics in APA-approved programs; of the 74 who returned usable data, 61 percent reported utilizing quantitative evaluation measures, and 35 percent reported no systematic evaluation procedures. Finally, Norcross, Stevenson, and Nash (1986) surveyed 179 APA-accredited internship programs and found that, like graduate training programs, internships depend primarily on informal qualitative procedures and secondarily on quantitative comparison procedures, with supervisors' evaluation of interns having the most weight in judging the quality of the internship. Relatedly, Ross and Altmaier (1989) take internship centers to task for continuing to employ intern selection criteria that have little or no demonstrated predictive validity either in internship sites or in other job sites, and they strongly recommend job analyses from which relevant selection criteria can be developed.

On a positive note, Stricker and Cohen (1984) and Stricker (1984) believe that psychology training programs are responding constructively to increased pressure to demonstrate accountability with efforts to implement quality assurance and peer review procedures. The critical accountability challenge for professional training programs has been to establish competency-based criteria to assess trainee proficiency in order to ensure high quality psychological services and to safeguard the welfare of the public. Bootzin and Ruggill (1988) outline several steps to meet this challenge: (1) develop clear operational definitions of clinical skills to be acquired; (2) specify measurable objectives for each training component or module; (3) determine trainee baseline skill levels; (4) carefully delineate the overall training process—who teaches what to whom by what means; and (5) utilize standardized quantitative measures of evaluation.

CURRENT OUTLOOK AND LOOKING AHEAD

In a married couple's reminiscence about changes they have witnessed in 20 years of professional psychology, Weiss and Weiss (1992) state:

> Training to be a psychologist appears to be a longer and more arduous process than it was 20 or 25 years ago. There are more requirements and more to learn. Students generally are more skilled and experienced by the time they receive their doctoral degree than we were. . . . The competition for going on an internship is much more formal and intense today. Not only do students have to work harder to become psychologists, there are more

requirements once they receive their degree before they
can become certified or licensed [p. 351].

On the other hand, some things about professional
training have stayed the same. There is still the issue of
maintaining a balance between research, scholarship, and
practice, which is as problematic today as it was 20 years
ago for probably different reasons. In a survey of 176 clinical psychology trainees from 16 APA-accredited Ph.D.
programs, Parker and Detterman (1988) found that the
majority expected to specialize in either clinical work or
research, with about 70 percent of the sample expecting
to concentrate most of their time on clinical practice; only
a minority planned to seek a career balanced between
research and practice. Across the 16 programs, training
seemed to have encouraged more of a clinical than a
research orientation, and "students become both more specialized in general and more clinically oriented in particular with training" (p. 344). As other writers have observed,
Parker and Detterman conclude that it is difficult to be
both a researcher and a clinician due to the continuing
tight job market for university positions, and to the fact
that the personality and aptitude of a large majority of
trainees tilt strongly toward either a research career or a
practice career.

> In an effort to integrate the two rival training models,
> Stricker (1992) argues that: our definition of science must
> expand beyond the narrow positivism that influenced much
> of our training. As we begin to appreciate the value of cre-
> ative approaches to knowledge generation, such as the use
> of qualitative research techniques, quasiexperimental de-
> signs, and case and other N = 1 studies, the scientist–
> practitioner model and the scholar–professional model will
> begin to blend into each other. The distinction between the
> scholar and the scientist is one of methodology; scholarship
> is the broader term, and the expansion of our appreciation
> of methodology reduces the distinction between the two
> [p. 548].

A fitting conclusion to Stricker's position is Peterson's (1991) statement: "Basic research, applied research, and professional work are all required, although it is absurd to expect the same people to do them all. We are likely to serve the public most effectively and to advance most rapidly as a discipline if basic scientists, applied scientists, and professionals work toward their separate goals in cooperative and complementary ways" (p. 429). It may have been Peterson who coined the phrase "consumers instead of doers of research" to refer to the position that trainees must be informed about research relevant to their professional education, be able to evaluate it (as well as their own practice methods) critically, and know how to translate research findings into practice.

The definition and purposes of professional training appear to be gaining clarification, albeit that there is not yet a strong discipline-wide consensus. The arbitrary distinctions placed on clinical, counseling, and school psychology have been tempered and naturally occurring overlap has been acknowledged. Nowhere is the overlap more evident than in the common core of scientific theory and methodology in the training curriculum. Given the overlap between clinical and counseling psychology, internships are no longer identified as either clinical or counseling.

This unification of clinical, counseling, and school psychology does not mean that each specialty does not or should not retain an unique identity. The separate integrity of each specialty field is retained in the professional core of the curriculum. At least this arrangement holds true for training programs that hew to the scientist–practitioner model. The Psy.D. and the few Ph.D. practitioner oriented programs accord somewhat more emphasis to the professional curriculum than to the scientific curriculum, and most of the psychologists in the field of training have come to terms with this sort of variation on the traditional model.

Still to be settled is the conflict between offering at the predoctoral level subspecialization in high priority societal need areas like AIDS, substance abuse, the elderly, varied minority populations, as well as high profile practice areas like clinical neuropsychology, behavioral medicine, family psychology, and on the other hand deferring all subspecialization to postdoctoral training or conventional on-the-job training. More will be said about this matter later.

To strengthen generic professional training and enhance the marketability of graduates, Beutler and Fisher (1994) present a persuasive rationale for replacing the traditional triad of specialty training with the "combined professional-scientific training," of which there are currently five fully or provisionally accredited programs (APA, 1993d).

There seems to be numerous irrefutable reasons to tout the advantages of this model over separate training in clinical, counseling, or school psychology. By providing minimal competency training in two or more of the current specialty fields (with subspecialization to be acquired at the postdoctoral level), graduates will: (1) be less disadvantaged in the flat, if not outright shrinking, job market; (2) have more diversified options for postdoctoral training; and (3) be more truly deserving of the status of being deemed a professional psychologist, since they will be closer to the concept of the human services provider envisioned by Levy (1984), Fox, Kovacs, and Graham (1985), Peterson (1991), Fox (1994), and many others.

A proactive agenda item has been, and will continue to be, to make the education and training of professional psychologists responsive to an increasingly pluralistic and culturally diverse society. All the national training conferences, beginning with the 1977 Vail Conference, have made a convincing argument "for broadening the cultural context of psychology training, education, research, and practice . . . for graduate programs to become more responsive to the diverse ethnic and cultural characteristics of the populations to be served by program graduates" (Hammond and Yung, 1993, p. 4). Given current demographic projections, Hammond and Yung conclude: "thus, to achieve a more appropriate representation, graduation rates of ethnic minority students would need to triple from their present level" (p. 3).

To progress further with the above agenda depends primarily on developing multicultural competency in all trainees (refer to Sue's, 1991, comprehensive model for cultural diversity training, cited in Highlen, 1994; see also APA, 1993a), and an improving recruitment and retention of minority graduate students and faculty. The APA Minority Locator Service can assist in the recruitment of students. Another source is the annual publication of Minority Undergraduate Students of Excellence (APA, 1993b). For faculty recruitment, a helpful source is the APA Office of Ethnic Minority Affairs; given its emphasis on developing minority staffed and minority-oriented internship centers (S. F. Schneider, 1981), it should indirectly assist in minority student and faculty recruitment and retention. Mention should also be made of APA's Minority Fellowship Program for beginning or full-time students in APA-accredited Ph.D. programs.

Within the discipline of psychology, the outlook for training in general and professional training in particular is promising. With the establishment of the APA Education Directorate, education and training are now on a par with the Science, Practice, and Public Interest Directorates within the structure of APA. In addition, work is underway to revise the accreditation guidelines and it is said that educational institutions and psychology departments will have a more influential voice both in the revision and in the implementation of new accreditation policy and standards (APA, 1994c). Further, a promising indication of more collaboration between the academics and the practitioners is the establishment of the Joint Council on Practitioner Education in Psychology (JCPEP), an organization of academics and practitioners committed to overseeing the education, training and licensure of professional psychologists.

On the other hand, *promising* would not be a fitting term to describe prospects for job market expansion and external funding. Except for certain high priority need areas, federal funds for training were sharply curtailed in the early 1980s (Stapp, Fulcher, and Wicherski, 1984; APA, 1986a), and the reduction in federal assistance, again with the exception of special targeted populations, has continued (Hammond and Yung, 1993).

Consistent with reduced federal training funds, there has been a declining percentage of trainees whose primary source of financial assistance comes from federal funds, as well as a declining percentage of trainees who receive nonfederal support (e.g., state funds). Thus, trainees have had to rely increasingly on personal resources to finance their professional education (Stapp et al., 1984; Hammond and Yung, 1993). This, of course, works against recruitment and especially retention of minority students (S. F. Schneider, 1981; Strickland, 1983b; Hammond and Yung, 1993).

The problematical time period is early on in training when a trainee does not yet possess the master's degree and requisite supervised experience, and when many programs insist on a full-time commitment to professional education. To finance the later years of training, a goodly number of doctoral trainees support themselves as part-time practitioners in community agencies and institutions; this is most often available only to those having a master's degree and one year of supervised experience, thereby (depending on the particular state's laws) qualifying for limited licensure. Another resource in later stages of training is to enter a military service program for professional psychology in order to fund the remainder of training.

The next two chapters deal with employment, but in the context of training, several points deserve mention. The unemployment rate for graduates has remained low since the previous decade. However, the fact that it does remain low, coupled with an increase in professional training programs and likely job reduction in the health care field as a consequence of more stringent cost containment policies, raises the specter of regulating the number of people to be trained as professional psychologists (Robiner, 1991). For one vigorous and one mild rebuttal to Robiner's conclusion of oversupply and need for "down-sizing," refer to VandenBos, DeLeon, and Belar (1991) and Pion (1991). But the most eloquent reply to Robiner belongs to S. F. Schneider (1991).

> How many psychologists are needed? Fewer of those practitioners who do not work with the underserved and whose numbers do not appreciably ameliorate the serious mental health problems of the nation. More, many more, who would provide services to the underserved, emphasize prevention, evaluation, and the empowerment of consumers. How many psychologists are needed? Fewer of those researchers whose work is correct, but timid and of limited importance. Many more whose research is potentially significant, near or at the cutting edge of science, and who are imaginative and mindful about application. It will be difficult to produce the psychologists who are needed without major modifications in our training and changes in the structure of incentives for practice and for research [p. 459].

Issues of employment and regulation (licensing) will receive detailed coverage in the later chapters.

As a final comment on training, Altman (1987) puts the problems and dilemmas of professional psychology into a longer-term, more sanguine perspective. He discusses the conflict, complementarity, and interplay of centripetal and centrifugal forces within the discipline of psychology as a whole. The centripetal represents the unifying and consolidating trends (which can also become reactionary and opposed to change), and the centrifugal represents the diverging and divisive trends (which can also be forward-looking and growth-producing). There is reason to believe that the profession will move forward to greater professional unification and productivity.

Chapter 5

Gaining Employment I: Basic Considerations

As a faculty member in a university department of psychology, it is common to have undergraduates seek counsel about what to do after receiving a bachelor's degree, what career to choose, how to get into graduate school, and employment opportunities. At this developmental stage, both personally and academically, the student typically wants specific information by which he or she can derive confidence that the future is bright. This often translates into hoping that the professor will issue a quasi-contract for lucrative employment in the field of psychology. Unfortunately, the employment situation today does not assure anyone of employment conditions in the future.

As this chapter was being written, an "advisee" sought an appointment and said the following:

> I just moved here from out of state. I majored in psychology and physical education and got decent grades in both areas. I would rather have been a high school coach, but my parents thought that I would more likely find a high-paying job in psychology, so I'm here. I still hope that a graduate degree in clinical psychology will allow me eventually to get a combined psychology–coaching position. I'm impressed with the university, but after being here two weeks, professors are telling me that a master's degree may not allow me to get a good job, and even if a job is open, there will be a lot of competition from the flood of

psychology majors, many with more training. I'm lonely away from home. I need to know for sure that meeting all of these demands will be worth it.

With such a plaintive tale, it would be satisfying to offer assurances, but that cannot be done. Instead, this chapter offers employment information to students like that advisee, with the hope that the information will be helpful for career planning.

Incidentally, the aforementioned advisee student went back home after the third week, and enrolled in a teacher education program at a hometown college. The advisee's departure should not be interpreted as indicating a bleak employment outlook per se. Rather, it reflects that graduate study must be predicated on personal decision making (e.g., not parental pressure), social–personal conditions (e.g., to avoid loneliness), and goals beyond an income (e.g., a career choice that fulfills multiple needs). One hopes that the advisee's choice to turn to teacher education, presumably to become a coach, will provide greater long-term gratification than the study of psychology, because the choice was made for more appropriate reasons than his proposed enrollment in psychology.

THE EMPLOYMENT SCENE

Gaining employment as a clinical psychologist is important both personally and professionally. On a personal level, it is obvious that no one would want to invest the time, money, energy, and identity in a career that would not yield reasonable dividends. On a professional level, the employment conditions indicate the status of the discipline and are crucial to assessing the short- and long-term employment potential.

Obviously, any student considering a career in clinical psychology must weigh many factors, of which the potential for obtaining employment is a major one. It is only fair to acknowledge that uncertainty exists for the future of psychologists. This is particularly true now that commercialized managed health care systems are in a dominant position, and there remains a foreboding of further health care reform. These and other economic and societal factors create questions about the future for all health care disciplines, and clinical psychology is no exception. At the same time, it is clear that health care will always be a high priority for our society, even though employment opportunities, conditions, and incomes will vary over time.

The specialty of clinical psychology has expanded in numbers of practitioners, scope of services, and employment settings. In his Presidential address to the American Psychological Association, Wiggins (1994) used the provocative title "Would You Want Your Child to Be a Psychologist?" and pointed out:

> Today, the APA has grown from fewer than 10,000 in 1952 to more than 120,000 members and affiliates. Psychologists are now licensed as autonomous professionals in all 50 states, the District of Columbia, and Puerto Rico. Most states have adopted freedom-of-choice legislation, which resulted in insurance carriers' defining psychologists as physicians for the treatment of nervous and mental disorders. Psychology has been incorporated in numerous state statutes, including commitment proceedings, child custody hearings, and a host of other state regulations, as well as Medicaid, worker compensation, and vocational rehabilitation programs [p. 465].

He notes that there are more practicing psychologists than psychiatrists, and a survey revealed psychology was fourth in the top 50 occupations with the brightest prospects for the beginning of the twenty-first century (behind computer systems analysis, physical therapy, and operations analysis, and well above law and medicine). "A new graduate with a doctoral degree in psychology can expect a salary from $28,000 to $55,000, depending on the area of training in psychology" (pp. 485–486). Wiggins sees a movement of psychology into primary health care (e.g., prescription privileges) as an opportunity to expand the scope of practice.

Along the same line, Fowler (1995), the chief executive officer of the APA, notes that in 1995 there are 132,000 members and affiliates of APA. Indicating that the incomes of psychologists overall have exceeded the rise in the cost of living, he says, "According to federal statistics, the median income of psychologists has increased by 44 percent over the past 10 years" (p. 3).

As a senior member of the profession, Weitz (1992) looks at the current state of affairs and recognizes that some voices cry that there are too many psychologists, but asserts, "We need at least 250,000 qualified psychological practitioners working full-time" (p. 452). Of great authority, the National Science Foundation (1988) reports: "Employment of psychologists is expected to increase at an above average growth rate through the year 2000. Between 1986 and 2000, civilian employment in psychology occupations is projected to increase between 27 percent and 39 percent; in contrast, the forecasted increase for all occupations ranges from 13 percent to 23 percent" (p. 3). These sources are cited to illustrate that clinicians and government alike recognize that there is, in fact, the possibility of clinical psychology continuing to be a growth industry.

Expansion of clinical psychology is not guaranteed; it will take considerable effort to achieve further growth in today's troubled economy. As will be evident subsequently, new roles for psychologists will likely increase job opportunities, particularly health care (Sleek, 1995b). Thus, adaptability on the part of the professional discipline and the practitioner will be important.

As new opportunities for employment occur, it will be essential for psychologists to educate the public, including other health care and human service professionals, about the benefits of psychological services. Meade (1994) says: "Psychology will not survive unless psychologists do a better job of letting the public know what the discipline is and why it is valuable" (p. 14). Similarly, Wiggins (1990) cautions that clinical psychology must be promoted by all concerned, which requires building a consensus between psychologists: "It is through public relation's promotion supplemented by the scientific knowledge of skilled clinicians that psychology can redefine itself in the changing health care market" (p. 52).

THE CLINICAL PSYCHOLOGIST'S JOB DESCRIPTION

Before reviewing the myriad factors that influence whether or not employment as a clinical psychologist can be gained, the basic job description should be considered. As might be expected, there is no single job description. Typically, the duties and functions are determined by the needs of the clientele, the objectives and resources of the employing facility, and the capabilities and preferences of the clinical psychologist. Moreover, commercialized managed health care systems and the health care reform movement have created ambiguity and shifts in priorities relevant to what services should be included in and emphasized by clinical psychology.

To posit a summary job description, consideration should be given to a statement from the American Psychological Association (undated):

> The clinical psychologist is educated and trained to generate and integrate scientific and professional knowledge and skills so as to further psychological science, the professional practice of psychology, and human welfare. Clinical psychologists are involved in research, teaching, and supervision, program development and evaluation, consultation, public policy, professional practice, and other activities that promote psychological health in

individuals, families, groups, and organizations. Their
work can range from prevention and early intervention
of minor problems and adjustment to dealing with the
adjustment and maladjustment of individuals whose
disturbance requires them to be institutionalized [page
unnumbered].

It is also pointed out that clinical psychologists may service persons at all developmental levels (i.e., infants
through older adults), individually or in groups, and in a
host of contexts: "Clinical psychologists work throughout
the United States in a variety of settings including individual practice, mental health service units, managed
health care organizations, hospitals, schools, universities,
industries, legal systems, medical systems, counseling
centers, governmental agencies, and military services"
(unnumbered).

In earlier years, it was possible to describe a typical
profile of clinical psychology services, but that is no longer
the case today.

EARLIER ROLE AND SERVICE
DEFINITION

Over the years, clinical psychology has passed through
several stages, with the emphases being on psychological
testing, insight-oriented counseling and psychotherapy, be-
haviorally oriented interventions, and eclectic or integra-
tive theoretical strategies.

Although clinical psychology in the 1990s and at the
advent of the twenty-first century is in a different situation
from the early 1980s, it is useful to look back to get an idea
about where the field seems to be going. Norcross and
Prochaska (1982b) surveyed a sample of members of the
American Psychological Association's (APA's) Division of
Clinical Psychology about particular professional activities
and found that the mean percentage of time spent in involvement with each activity was as follows: psychotherapy,

34.7 percent; diagnosis and assessment, 13.2 percent; teaching, 12.0 percent; supervision (clinical), 8.5 percent; research, 7.9 percent; consultation, 7.5 percent; administration, 13.4 percent; and other, 2.9 percent. It should be noted that every clinical psychologist was not necessarily involved in all of these activities. The involvement percentages were: psychotherapy, 88.3 percent; diagnosis and assessment, 73.8 percent; teaching, 61.7 percent; supervision (clinical), 73.7 percent; research, 52.8 percent; consultation, 67.4 percent; administration, 61.6 percent; and other, 12.2 percent.

Analyzing theoretical orientation, Norcross and Prochaska (1982a) found the following alignments: learning theory-behavior, 14.40 percent; cognitive, 6.26 percent; humanistic, 1.68 percent; psychodynamic, 30.05 percent; Rogerian, 3.14 percent; Sullivanian, 2.29 percent; existential, 1.46 percent; systems, 4.18 percent; eclectic, 30.89 percent; and other, 5.64 percent. When they considered the number of years of experience, they found that there were shifts in the percentage, with the inexperienced group being more oriented toward behavioral and cognitive psychology and less psychodynamically oriented; they speculate that "it is possible that as clinicians become more experienced, they may gravitate toward a more psychodynamic orientation" (p. 6). The percentage of time devoted to therapy activities according to treatment format were: individual therapy, 63.5 percent; group therapy, 7.3 percent; marital-couples therapy, 11.5 percent; family therapy, 9.0 percent; and behavior modification, 7.1 percent (Norcross and Prochaska, 1982b). Although these percentages, revealing the alignments with theories and formats, are from a decade-plus ago, there is no reason to believe that there have been appreciable changes to date. It may well be, however, that the contemporary and future conditions for practice will bring about shifts, such as toward more group services for medical conditions (Sleek, 1995a).

CURRENT ROLE AND SERVICE DEFINITION

As mentioned, the roles and services for clinical psychology are traveling an uncharted course. Phares (1992) says: "Clinical psychology is a profession in flux and ferment. Although clinical psychology retains its basic mission of applying psychological principles to the adjustment of individuals, the methods and the professional framework by which it seeks to accomplish this are undergoing change" (p. 27). Public policy, as it determines legal and economic conditions, is in a constant state of flux, and the roles and services of virtually all health care providers, including clinical psychology, change direction with societal, political, and economic winds.

For actual services, it seems likely that traditional clinical psychological assessment and treatment techniques and strategies will continue, perhaps with degrees of emphasis quite different than in the past. Nietzel, Bernstein, and Milich (1994) acknowledge that no definition of clinical psychology exists, because, "the field has been expanding in so many different directions that any attempt to capture it in a sentence or two is bound to be too vague, too narrow, or soon outdated" (p. 2). Nonetheless, they conclude: "It is probably fair to say that 95% of all clinical psychologists spend their working lives engaged in some combination of six activities: assessment, treatment, research, teaching, consultation, and administration" (p. 4).

Commercialized managed health care systems and health care reform have created all sorts of unprecedented challenges, problems, and opportunities. Meade (1994) notes a trend "toward larger corporations supplying a wide range of medical services, more use of master's-level psychologists to provide therapy, less one-on-one therapy, more group therapy and more preventive services, such as stress-management programs and parenting groups" (p. 14). With decision making about roles and services being made by corporate executives or governmental regulators, it is incontrovertible that the criteria for quality (be it for practitioners or their services) and the priorities (what will determine use of financial resources) will be considerably different from what clinicians, with their dedication to professionalism and scientist–practitioner standards, have been accustomed to in the recent past. Certainly there is considerably more emphasis on cost containment at the present time than at any time in the past (Schulman, 1988), and given federal health care priorities, it seems likely that cost containment and accountability imposed on health care providers, including clinical psychologists, will increase in the future (Starr, 1994).

The ambiguity of the roles and services for clinical psychology should not be viewed as a harbinger of doom or a reason for not entering the profession. To the contrary, change can be constructive, and certainly for human services, such as clinical psychology, it is both unavoidable and essential in order for advances in professionalism to take place. Instead of gloom and doom, it would seem that would-be clinical psychologists (as well as those already in the field) should adopt a positive view. As Phares (1992) says, "the current situation offers an unparalleled opportunity to participate in shaping the future of a profession" (p. 27).

EMPLOYMENT SATISFACTION

The dividends from a career are, of course, far more than only financial. There must be a sense of personal satisfaction derived from one's work, otherwise both the service recipients (e.g., the clients or patients, coworkers, supervisors, and ultimately society itself) and the worker will suffer negative consequences. Lack of job satisfaction results in a poor work product (e.g., lessened quality of service); faulty functioning (e.g., poor motivation to perform or to develop improved skills); and illness (e.g., mental difficulties, such as depression, anxiety, and obsessions, and physical difficulties, such as stress-related disorders). While the foregoing descriptions may seem rather "industrial" in nature, they do, in fact, apply to professional employment as well. Certainly, a dissatisfied clinical psychologist is going to be less productive than one who does find satisfaction.

Job satisfaction makes a much needed contribution to the person's sense of social worthiness, self-esteem, and ego structure. In turn, these intrapersonal qualities influence mightily the qualities that the person experiences interpersonally, such as the degree to which he or she can be a healthy member of a family and a community. Clinical psychology certainly holds the potential of yielding powerful personal benefits, such as from the respectability and esteem granted to members of the profession.

Although money is not the whole story, the importance of income should not be denied. In this day and age, it is naive, if not ignorant, to assert that a clinical psychologist, or any other professional in health and human services, should be altruistic to the point of extreme self-sacrifice. There was a time in our societal evolution when a professional could, in fact, experience considerable reward from helping others. The priorities of society were such that there was social recognition and, thus, reward for altruistic behavior in serving the needs of others and placing this commitment well above such personal needs as income. With the changes in societal values and an economy that mandates concern about income in order to survive (literally and figuratively), the potential benefits from the altruism have diminished. With clinical psychology, however, considerable financial and altruistic benefits remain.

To be concerned about profit should not be viewed as greed. Pay is endemic to overall organizational functioning. In other words, the profit dimension of, say, a mental health facility relates in many ways to the services and operations: "At this point, it is sufficient to say that pay systems in organizations are closely linked to the following major aspects of organizations: superior-subordinate relationships, job design, organizational structure, organizational climate, management training and development, information and control systems, performance appraisal, and management philosophy or style" (Lawler, 1981, p. 8). If we apply these organizational aspects to clinical psychology, it is readily apparent that it would be ill-advised to ignore the financial dimension.

Consideration of pay should acknowledge that the number of dollars per se is seldom the whole story. The very nature of pay creates a perceptual set in the minds of the employee. Lawler (1981) tells us:

1. Satisfaction with a reward is a function of how much is received and how much the individual feels should be received [p. 12].
2. People's feelings of satisfaction are influenced by comparisons with what happens to others [p. 12].
3. People often misperceive the rewards of others [p. 14].
4. Overall job satisfaction is influenced by how satisfied employees are with both the intrinsic and extrinsic rewards they receive from their jobs [p. 15].

Reeves and Torrez (1994) highlight the somewhat mystical nature of pay, saying: "Worker paychecks assume symbolic or mythical meanings quite apart from the rational figures neatly printed on these paychecks. A paycheck is also a symbol of status in society and among one's peers" (p. 147).

Thus, the clinical psychologist will be mindful of the amount of income and will evaluate its adequacy according to, among other things, the investment that he or she was required to make in order to become a clinical psychologist. As is clear throughout this book, the investment in terms of the years of education and training required is considerable. Therefore, there is no apology for recognizing that clinical psychologists should aggressively seek to maximize financial rewards.

If public policy priorities downgrade the importance of mental health services (as the recent health care reform trend seems to support), there may well be fewer mental health facilities, fewer job opportunities, and a diminution of intrinsic and extrinsic rewards for being a mental health professional. If this occurs, it is only logical that the clinical psychologist will be dissatisfied with a variety of employment conditions, not the least of which will be the amount of pay.

It must be acknowledged that some clinical psychologists have grown dissatisfied with the field. This dissatisfaction may, however, be explained by conditions other than employment or income per se. For example, it is a truism that managed health care has, in general, resulted in a decreased hourly rate for therapeutic services, which has led some clinical psychologists to remember "the good old days" and refuse to provide services for the reduced rate. Also, there are master's-level practitioners in other disciplines (e.g., social work and mental health counseling) who are now eligible for, among other things, third-party payments (e.g., from an Employee Assistance Program), which diminishes the income of the more highly trained clinical psychologist. Consequently, a number of clinical psychologists have concluded that they should abandon clinical services and either use their psychological skills in other ways or, perhaps for existential reasons, take on nonpsychological jobs (psychologists have chosen to sell real estate, develop computer software, run campgrounds, operate restaurants and bookstores, or market "home products").

Dissatisfaction may relate to the length of time that a person has been a clinical psychologist. Walfish, Polifka, and Stenmark (1985) found that recent graduates of clinical psychology training programs have a high level of satisfaction, but older, more experienced clinical psychologists express a greater degree of career dissatisfaction.

In a survey of psychology graduates with master's, specialist's, and related degrees (subdoctoral degrees), Gehlmann (1994) concluded that, "Generally speaking, the majority of graduates were satisfied with their current occupational level" (p. 7). In a similar study of recent doctoral degree recipients, Kohout and Wicherski (1991) report:

> The majority of doctorates seemed to be fairly satisfied with their current positions. With the exception of opportunities for promotion and salary to some extent, over two thirds of the new doctorates were satisfied or very satisfied with benefits, opportunities for personal development and recognition, supervisor, co-workers and working conditions. Interestingly, factors that might be called external to one's control (e.g., supervisor, co-workers and working conditions) were rated more highly than the remaining, more personal factors, such as benefits, salary, recognition, personal development, and opportunities for promotion [p. 8].

The availability of particular kinds of jobs fluctuates according to innumerable social and economic factors, and clinical psychologists are not immune to changes in social priorities and the consequent rise and fall of available jobs.

It is important not to set one's sights on a single kind of position or type of service. At one point, the highest status for a clinical psychologist was to be a professor (and the more prestigious the university, the better) and/or an upper-level clinician in a well-financed public or private mental health facility. As community mental health programs dwindled, establishing a solid private practice became a preference, followed by serving in a medical setting (either as a full-time salaried staff member or a part-time independent contractor).

Certainly university, private practice, and hospital-based roles remain desirable and probably the most likely sources of employment. Unfortunately, societal conditions are such that the wise clinical psychologist should be prepared to apply his or her professional skills in employment contexts and roles that have heretofore been uncommon. That is, there must be a readiness to make adaptations of professional skills and aspirations, and seek employment in nontraditional settings. As she cleverly explores how "New Ph.D.'s Can Find a Life Outside Academe," Hotaling (1994) quips, "'Social-Science Ph.D. to Run Major Corporation' is a headline I fervently hope to read someday on the front page of *The New York Times*—proving that you don't have to drive a cab if you've got a Ph.D. and can't find a tenure-track job" (p. B-2).

The consequences must not be minimized of trying a profession and, if dissatisfied, moving on. The negative fallout of job dissatisfaction and of leaving a profession is great. Not only has the person chosen to cut short a career in which he or she has made a substantial personal investment, but society loses a valuable professional resource. The lost resource will have to be replenished through additional investments of personal and public resources, which could otherwise be spent in improving other qualities for life. Thus, choosing to become a clinical psychologist must be made on the basis of solid knowledge of the issues.

CAREER DEVELOPMENT

Schein (1978) captures the essence of a career development perspective:

> (1) the problem of improving human resource planning and development activities in organizations; (2) the problem of improving individual career planning and helping people who are caught in difficult work situations to cope more effectively with those situations; (3) the problem of improving the matching process at all stages of the career so that early-, mid-, and late-career crises can be dealt with more effectively by both the organization and the individuals caught in these crises; (4) the problem of

obsolescence, demotivation, and leveling off which occurs in mid- and late-career; (5) the problem of balancing family and work concerns at different life stages; and (6) the problem of maintaining the productivity and motivation of all those employees who are individual contributors and/or who are not motivated toward climbing the organizational ladder [p. 2].

Too few students give careful thought to this array of issues at the time they make their decision to major in psychology, or when they vest much of their life (and the lives of their family members) in entering graduate studies in clinical psychology. The basic notion is, no doubt, that the longer one is in a career, the wiser one becomes and the more employment opportunities will be available. This is a logical notion, but it is contradicted by fact. Indeed, discrimination against the worker (including the professional) over the age of 40 has been and continues to be extreme (notwithstanding that the Age Discrimination in Employment Act offers legal safeguards to persons between the ages of 40 and 70).

Age discrimination comes in many forms. To illustrate how it enters into the employment of clinical psychologists, consider the following two situations.

A clinical psychologist has been employed by the federal government for all of his or her career, spanning some 25 years. During that time, he or she has published award-winning research, given leadership within the employing unit (such as serving as director), and achieved prominence (such as through participation on several blue-ribbon committees that charted national and international health policies, and having been elected president of several national mental health organizations). Stated simply, the clinical psychologist has given about half of his or her life to one employer—a government mental health unit—and has achieved what most clinical psychologists would consider to be the ultimate career goals. However, the government, presumably because of shifts in public policy priorities, stripped away support for mental health services when this clinical psychologist was 52 years old. Reportedly, an executive branch analysis led to the conclusion that senior mental health professionals in the government should be encouraged to take early retirement, thereby freeing up their salary monies to either hire beginning professionals at lower salaries or to allocate the monies to another sector, say defense. If a senior mental health professional resisted the idea of early retirement, efforts would be made to reassign him or her to an undesirable position, one that might carry the same salary but would remove the previously enjoyed intrinsic benefits (such as status, creativity, and the like) and would inflict new, negative demands (such as performing routine, rigidly scheduled functions).

The not so honorable objective is easy to recognize: if the employment conditions produce job dissatisfaction, the senior mental health professional would be pressured toward early retirement, and the administrative goal of freeing up salary monies would be obtained. It should be added that essentially this same scenario is known to have occurred in any number of other settings, including universities and hospitals. Stated simply, services provided by a senior person can be obtained more cheaply by hiring a more junior person and/or downgrading or eliminating the position.

As a second example, consider a clinical psychologist employed by a state university as a professor. The professor has been with the university for 25 years, is 52 years old, teaches three classes each semester, publishes regularly in scholarly journals, holds certain honors (such as having been named a diplomate in clinical psychology by the American Board of Professional Psychology), and earns $60,000 per year.

If the professor taught at the most esteemed "flagship campus" in the state's university system, it is probable that the salary would be considerably higher (say by

$10,000 or more), than if he or she performed the same functions at a secondary campus in the same university system. If the professor were female, it is probable (at least historically) that her salary would be significantly lower than the salaries of her male counterparts.

Suppose that the professor decides that his or her career needs—which include being more productive professionally—could be better met by seeking employment at another university. Applications are sent out, and despite strong professional credentials, nothing but rejections are received. Why should this be so? Place yourself in the position of the chairperson of the psychology department at the hiring institution. If $60,000 had been allocated to the department to improve the clinical psychology training program, you could afford to hire this particular professor, but for the same amount of money, you could afford to hire two beginning professors and thereby double the number of courses that would be taught and double the number of new faculty members in the program (with all the side benefits of having two for the price of one, such as more advisement of students, greater variety of research interests, and so on).

Sometimes the decision to avoid senior professors is for reasons other than money. For example, a clinical psychology training program might contain behaviorists, proponents of psychoanalysis, and others who believe that a health psychology (including psychopharmacology) model is more important than a therapy model. When it comes time to hire a new professor, each faction champions its preferences. While compromises and negotiations usually occur, they may be predicated on the premise that "If I'm going to give in and support hiring your candidate, I want to be sure that he or she is potentially open to my preferences." Age discrimination enters in because senior professors are perceived, probably rightly, as having mind-set positions on professional issues and as being less malleable than younger professors.

Thus, the student should also give thought to his or her long-range needs and the employment issues that are likely to be encountered, to the extent that it is possible. At some point, say 10 years into one's career, the possibility of moving to another position later in life will be difficult (assuming that societal priorities for mental health services remain somewhat like what they are today).

A clear-cut example of unpredictable trends in employment of clinical psychologists is found in the community mental health movement. During the administrations of John F. Kennedy and Lyndon B. Johnson, there was great public support for mental health services. The Joint Commission on Mental Illness and Health (1961) gave impetus to the establishment of many community-based facilities, and employment of all types of mental health professionals was readily available. Clinical psychology training programs added courses in community concepts, particularly mental health consultation. Some training programs changed their designations from "clinical" to "community-clinical" psychology. Then came a change in political orientation, and during the Nixon administration the continuing trend away from publicly supported mental health services began. Today's economic priorities do not favor mental health funding. Consequently, some employment opportunities have diminished, particularly in the community mental health arena.

There is an even more critical message that the student of psychology should heed. Society often shifts its priorities, whether they be witnessed in decisions made by the executive branch of the federal government or those recruiting faculty members for a university. Many of these shifts will fulfill the old adage of "Robbing Peter to pay Paul." A priority will perhaps shift away from mental health services and toward lower taxes for reasons that may be of dubious long-range benefit. Not only will this inflict unforeseen, unjust, and hurtful conditions on the individual, such as depriving a clinical psychologist of employment opportunities, it will have an equally or greater hurtful effect on society itself. Shifting priorities are part of the nature of a democratic society. Public policy does shift, and often the shifts may not be in the best interest of anything but short-term gains.

PREREQUISITES FOR EMPLOYMENT

As a profession, clinical psychology adheres to a set of ethics, known as the "Ethical Principles of Psychologists and Code of Conduct" (APA, 1992a). Ethics serve many purposes, such as promulgating standards for professional conduct that will safeguard those who are served by psychologists and advance the profession. Even the latter purpose has a public service core. A strong profession will lead to an upgrading of standards for its members, and will lead to higher quality services for clients.

The "Ethical Principles of Psychologists and Code of Conduct" represents the views of the APA. The ethics apply to its members, but there are other psychologists who are not APA members and who are, technically, not bound by those ethics. However, APA standards are generally considered the "prevailing" standards, even to the point that the statutes in some states make explicit reference to them or, more subtly, use them implicitly as a frame of reference for regulatory legal functions (e.g., the decisions rendered in disciplinary actions conducted by a state licensing board for psychologists). In this way, APA ethics are potentially applicable to all who would practice as psychologists, whether or not they are APA members.

On the issue of competence for employment as a psychologist, the APA ethics prescribe as follows:

> Principle A: Competence. Psychologists strive to maintain high standards in their work. They recognize the boundaries of their particular competencies and the limitations of their expertise. They provide only those services and use only techniques for which they are qualified by education,

training, and experience. Psychologists are cognizant of the fact that the competencies required in serving, teaching, and/or studying groups of people vary with the distinctive characteristics of those groups. In those areas in which recognized professional standards do not yet exist, psychologists exercise careful judgment and take appropriate precautions to protect the welfare of those with whom they work. They maintain knowledge of relevant scientific and professional information related to the services they render, and they recognize the need for ongoing education. Psychologists make appropriate use of scientific, professional, technical, and administrative resources [p. 1599].

This ethical posture spawns several prerequisites for employment as a clinical psychologist; let us consider three examples.

First, the would-be clinical psychologist must have the qualifications endorsed by the profession. He or she cannot self-ordain readiness for employment.

Second, even when the prerequisite of academic training has been met, the would-be clinical psychologist is restrained from seeking employment that might involve techniques or skills that have not been adequately mastered. For example, there are certain types of patients who require highly specialized therapeutic interventions that few trainees emerging from a Ph.D. or Psy.D. program would be prepared to provide (particularly without the wisdom of a more experienced supervisor), yet some employers (e.g., those more concerned about cost containment than quality of service) might be open to hiring a new Ph.D. or Psy.D. holder for such work. Ethically, the fledgling clinical psychologist cannot accept such a decision by the employer.

Third, the matter of competence is never fulfilled. It is much like seeking self-actualization: great progress can be made with clear-cut evidence of accomplishments, but this only opens the potential for new vistas. In employment, remaining in the same job carries the responsibility of growing with the job—if the employment is to be ethical, there can be no stagnation.

The starting point for employment is academic training. There will be career opportunities for students with an undergraduate major in psychology (such as in business, schools, the military, and community health and welfare programs). The term *clinical psychologist* is reserved for those with advanced and specialized graduate training. The term *clinical psychology* now refers to clinical services, which may be provided by psychologists with diverse academic "majors" or backgrounds (notably aligned with clinical, counseling, or school psychology). At this point in time, the standard for the specialty certainly requires possessing a doctorate from a regionally accredited institution, along with certain other qualifications (e.g., courses in particular areas and qualified supervised experiences).

While there is reason to believe that job opportunities for persons with undergraduate psychology training are actually expanding, it is interesting to note that "At the baccalaureate level, however, there has been a sharp decline" (National Science Foundation, 1988, p. 3). In addition to other careers having gained in attractiveness, the decline in undergraduate majors in psychology may be due to the fact that employment opportunities in the area of clinical psychology tend to be greatly restricted unless the applicant has an accredited doctorate.

Regardless, clinical psychology does afford career opportunities for persons without a doctorate, such as those with a bachelor's or master's degree and certain relevant coursework and training. With current licensing laws, however, when working without a doctorate and the mandatory licensing, the nondoctoral person commonly must be an "assistant" or "technician" under the direct supervision of the senior clinical psychologist. DeLuca and Putnam (1993) state: "The use of the professional/ technician model has become an integrated part of the health care delivery system. . . . The employment of nondoctoral-level (e.g., bachelor-degree level) technicians by neuropsychologists and, to a lesser extent, by clinical psychologists, is also a historical and long-established tradition" (p. 100). They underscore the appropriateness of this technical model for administering and scoring psychological tests.

In some states, nondoctoral persons may be licensed as school psychologists for independent practice, and some provide for the restricted licensure of, for example, a limited licensed psychologist. There is an emerging effort by master's level psychologists to promote legislation that would accommodate their services (note the formation of the North American Association of Masters in Psychology). While early in the process, it seems reasonable to anticipate that commercialized managed health care will support legislation for and services by subdoctoral psychologists.

Erdwins and Buffardi (1983) found that nondoctoral psychologists have restricted roles, but do engage in psychological testing and therapy, and are generally satisfied with their duties. Perlman's (1985) survey of master's level clinical psychologists reveals: (1) they maintain a strong identity with clinical practice (about 50% of their time is spent providing psychotherapy); (2) they have noteworthy dissatisfaction with their training (over one-fourth express some dissatisfaction with their overall graduate training); and (3) "The doctoral psychologist engages in a wider array of activities (greater role variety) . . ." (p. 563).

Without a proper doctoral degree, the would-be psychologist is denied recognition by or acceptance into the profession of psychology. At a minimum, membership in the APA requires, in summary, a doctoral degree from a program that was primarily psychological in content (and included a psychological dissertation) and conferred by a graduate or professional school that is regionally accredited. While there are limited exceptions (such as for degrees awarded outside of the United States), it means that:

(1) a Ph.D. degree from a program that was not primarily psychological in content, no matter what the recipient's personal qualities nor how prestigious the university, would not suffice for membership; and (2) the fast track of a "store bought" Ph.D. degree, such as from one of the commercial purveyors of doctorates, would not fulfill the degree requirement. To be legitimate, the academic psychological training must be through a university, college, or professional school that is accredited by the U.S. Office of Education and a recognized regional accreditation board (see later comments about the institutional accreditation requirements maintained by the Florida Board of Psychological Examiners). Note that being licensed by the state department of education to be a training program, as is the case with many of the "store bought" degree sources, is insufficient.

It is feasible that a legitimate doctoral degree in one area of psychology can be used to gain employment in another area of psychology. For example, a psychologist who was a member of the APA and who held a Ph.D. degree in experimental psychology from the psychology department of a highly respected university found that he could not obtain employment. Finally, he was hired by a state hospital for the mentally ill as a clinical psychologist. Although this was legal, it was probably not ethical because he had no specialized training in such areas as psychological testing and psychotherapy, and had never received supervision for the clinical services that he provided. Fortunately, he recognized the dilemma that the financial stress to support his family had created, and he immediately arranged for a senior professor of clinical psychology to supervise his work (at his own expense!) and enrolled in clinical psychology courses.

This attempted remedy, sometimes referred to as "back dooring" into clinical psychology, is not recommended. The specialty of clinical psychology has carefully established standards. Moreover, the importance, dominance, and uniformity of state licensing laws make it increasingly difficult and unwise to attempt to "back door" one's way into the specialty.

There are, however, appropriate ways for someone with training in a nonclinical area of psychology to capitalize on the previous preparation and move into clinical psychology, as might be necessitated by shifting priorities of public policy that dictate employment opportunities. Even some of the most stringent state licensing laws provide the opportunity for augmentation of education. For example, Florida Board of Psychological Examiners (1995) provides an Augmentation of Education rule (59AA-14.001):

> It is the intent in this rule chapter to provide a mechanism whereby an applicant, who has graduated from a doctoral program with a major in psychology, which is not fully comparable to the standard of training in an American Psychological Association approved program, may augment education in order to qualify for licensure by examination. . . . The Board, recognizing that supplemental education through a piecemeal or self-directed course of study is not acceptable, adopts a formal mechanism provided by this rule chapter as an acceptable method of augmenting education [p. 2105].

The rule goes on to specify: criteria for being eligible to pursue augmentation (e.g., a doctoral degree with a major in psychology from a university or professional school accredited by one of the regional accrediting bodies recognized by the Council on Postsecondary Accreditation, or publicly recognized as a member in good standing with the Association of Universities and Colleges or Canada, etc., but not a degree-mill doctorate); and what the augmentation must involve and how this will be documented. There must be coursework in particular areas, namely biological bases of behavior, cognitive-affective bases of behavior, social bases of behavior, individual behavior, scientific and professional ethics and standards, research design and methodology, statistics, psychological measurements, and history and systems of psychology.

This "augmentation" or "retreading" approach does not allow for catch-as-catch-can supervision and coursework. Rather, it means having a properly qualified clinical trainer tailor a sequence of training experiences which will, for all practical purposes, provide the psychologist with a "second major." That is, he or she will have comprehensive training, say, in both experimental psychology and clinical psychology.

GUIDELINES FOR SPECIALIZATION

In 1977, the APA's Council of Representatives adopted the first generic set of guidelines for psychological service delivery. Soon thereafter, the Council adopted specialty guidelines. These are set forth by the APA's Committee on Professional Standards (1981) as the "Specialty Guidelines for the Delivery of Service," and contain separate sets of detailed standards for each of the following four specialties: (1) clinical psychology; (2) counseling psychology; (3) industrial–organizational psychology; and (4) school psychology.

The guidelines hold that the practices in these four specialties necessitate particular skills and competencies:

> Traditionally, all learned disciplines have treated the designation of specialty practice as a reflection of preparation in greater depth in a particular subject matter, together with a voluntary limiting of focus to a more restricted area of practice by the professional. Lack of specialty designation does not preclude general providers of psychological services from using the methods or dealing with the populations of any specialty, except insofar as psychologists voluntarily refrain from providing services they are not trained to render. It is the intent of these Guidelines, however, that after the grandparenting period, psychologists not put themselves forward as *specialists* in a given area

unless they meet the qualifications noted in the Guidelines. . . . [p. 640].

The specialty guidelines were structured to recognize
legal authority (e.g., statutory licensure), govern the
quality of services in both the private and public sectors,
endorse levels of training and experience, and foster accountability.

In 1981, the would-be clinical psychologist would need
to acknowledge the service scope of the specialty guidelines:
"Clinical psychological services refers to the application of
principles, methods, and procedures for understanding, predicting, and alleviating intellectual, emotional, psychological, and behavioral disability and discomfort. Direct services
are provided in a variety of health settings, and direct and
supportive services are provided in the entire range of social, organizational, and academic institutions and agencies" (APA, 1981, p. 642).

Clinical psychology services included psychodiagnostics, therapeutic interventions, professional consultation,
program development, supervision, and evaluation, as
would be relevant to the clinical context. The 1981 specialty guidelines for clinical psychology specified amongst
other things the organizational elements necessary for
clinical psychology services, such as how long records should
be kept, when and how supervision should be provided,
and so on.

It is possible that an employer might maintain a clinical organization that would satisfy the standards of another profession, say psychiatry, but would fail to uphold
the standards for clinical psychology. For example, known
incidents include a nonpsychologist administrator want-
ing a psychologist to prepare a diagnostic report with data
that were inadequate by accepted psychological standards;
attempting to denigrate the confidentiality of psychological records; and offering a psychologist a pad of medical
prescriptions already signed by a physician, to be issued

at the discretion of the psychologist. According to the 1981 specialty guidelines, the clinical psychologist should not subvert the professional standards of his or her discipline in deference to those of another profession in an employing organization.

Analysis of the standards for specialization in clinical psychology has not stopped with the 1981 guidelines; it is a continuing task. The APA's Board of Professional Affairs (1984b) sponsored a Subcommittee on Specialization, which asserted that specialization should develop from a scientific core; from this foundation, applied generic cores of proficiencies, knowledge, and skills for a specialty can emerge.

In subsequent years, clinical psychology has become firmly aligned with the scientist–practitioner model, that is, the premise that any clinical specialization must rest on a behavioral science foundation. DeGroot (1994b) describes the emphasis given to putting science into clinical education by the Council of University Directors of Clinical Psychology. B. N. Phillips (1989) identifies a collaborative relationship between researchers and clinicians: "Through such collaboration, researchers are apt to ask better research and application questions, use research procedures that have greater external validity, and interpret and apply their findings to practice more successfully. Practitioners, through such collaboration, are likely to understand and appreciate more fully the strengths and limitations of their own practice" (p. 7).

Considerable strength for the view has been due to the movement of clinical psychology toward health care. For example, the practice of psychology in hospital settings is fertile for allowing consumers access to behavior science knowledge: "In general medical and surgical hospitals, there is growing demand for psychological consultation from the emergency room to the delivery room" (Enright, Resnick, DeLeon, Sciara, and Tanney, 1990, p. 1061). Also, by becoming members of the health care team, psychologists are finding new roles (Sleek, 1995b).

With the open doors for new service settings, such as hospitals, there is renewed interest in specialty training for clinical psychologists. DeGroot (1994a) reports on the Joint Interim Committee for the Identification and Recognition of Specialties and Proficiencies within APA, which is designed to explore the possibility of promoting additional specialties beyond clinical, counseling, school, and industrial-organizational psychology. Under this rubric, a "specialty" would be a service that necessitated advanced knowledge and skills, cultivated and acquired by an organized sequence of education and training. A "proficiency" would be a circumscribed service domain aligned with a demonstrated public need and recognized by the profession.

It is noteworthy that the notion of promoting additional specialties or declaring proficiencies is not uniformly supported. Buetler and Fisher (1994) believe that counseling, clinical, and school psychology have always had more in common than they have had differences, and assert that: "More current developments in the workplace and expanding arenas of interests among students, however, have made this traditional model outdated" (p. 68). They posit that: "The combined specialty-training model, coupled with postdoctoral training, may both better meet the needs of students whose interests cross the traditional distinctions among the specialties and better address the needs of a society whose need for special skills and knowledge is shifting much of the burden of subspecialization training to the postdoctoral years" (p. 68). Relatedly, Matarazzo (1987) endorses that there is "only one psychology, no specialties"; and:

> The history of clinical psychology, health psychology, and neuropsychology (and, I might add, experimental, social, physiological, or industrial/organizational psychology)

leaves little question in my mind that each area for the potential, fee-for-service postdoctoral application of generic psychology has developed some unique proficiencies and also that, by 1987, each thus has achieved, along with its recognition as a research specialty, a fair amount of de facto recognition as a postdoctoral professional specialty [p. 902].

The important message to the psychology student considering employment possibilities is that the specialty of clinical psychology is not in its permanent form. For the student who will not enter the job market for several more years, the specific prerequisites for employment as a clinical psychologist may not yet be available. For example, there may be alternative routes to training in clinical psychology besides the traditional clinical psychology program (e.g., counseling psychology or school psychology). Also, there may be other specialties available in the very near future (e.g., psychopharmacology is certainly emerging rapidly as a clinical option for psychologists), and employment as a traditional clinical psychologist may not be the number one preference

TRAINING PROGRAMS ACCREDITED BY THE APA

As discussed in earlier chapters, the APA's Committee on Accreditation (1994c) accredits doctoral training programs, processing applications from programs in the traditional specialties of clinical, counseling, and school psychology (and programs that combine more than one of the traditional specialties), as well as programs in emerging areas of professional specialization. Further, the Committee is preparing to accredit postdoctoral training programs that prepare psychologists for delivery of services requiring specialized advanced training in an area of professional psychology.

Not all doctoral training programs in clinical psychology have earned accredited status from the APA Committee on Accreditation. Thus, being "APA accredited" is a status symbol, which enhances funding opportunities for the program's research and training endeavors, and elevates graduates' competitiveness in the job market. On the latter, many employers, particularly those who honor high standards for the provision of clinical psychology services or wish to enhance the status of their employing institution, seek employees who are graduates of fully or provisionally approved training programs. Being from an APA-approved training program is a valuable asset, one that will facilitate gaining and maximizing employment.

It has long been difficult to gain admission to doctoral study in psychology, particularly in clinical psychology. Note that, at most training institutions, admission standards for counseling psychology and school psychology are comparable to those for clinical psychology.

More than two decades ago, Nyman (1973) found that the odds were greater against admission to a clinical psychology program than for admission to medical school. It seems likely that today the odds against admission are at least as great or even greater than in 1973, particularly if admission is sought to an APA-accredited program (be it in clinical, counseling, or school psychology).

Accreditation has direct relevance to employment. As already stated, some employers (especially now that the job market is shrinking) give preference to psychologists from APA-accredited programs. Moreover, there is reason to believe that state licensing boards are moving in the direction of requiring that applicants for licensure be from APA-accredited programs or their equivalent (with the equivalency having to be authoritatively documented).

There are, of course, many fine clinical psychology training programs, including those in prestigious universities, that do not have APA accreditation. The odds of being admitted to a training program that does not hold APA accreditation may or may not be better. The training may be excellent, and job opportunities may be plentiful for the graduates. The only message is that having a degree from an APA-accredited program is a positive attainment.

Chapter 6

Gaining Employment II: Understanding the Selection System

Once the trainee has acquired the qualifications necessary for entering the specialty of clinical psychology, it is time to cope with the conditions that govern the existing job market. For the graduate, there has been an untold investment of time, energy, and money in the quest to become an employed professional. In a perfect society, the doors to employment should be wide open, ready to receive any qualified graduate and to heap rewards for dedicated service. Of course, it is not a perfect society, but it is the best available, and the opportunity exists to succeed in the chosen profession. While there are certain conditions today that may make employment in any health care field seem doubtful, in point of fact there is a reason to be optimistic, especially in clinical psychology.

INTERDISCIPLINARY COMPETITION FOR EMPLOYMENT

Clinical psychologists (including those who have majored in clinical, counseling, or school psychology) enter a job market that is also open to psychiatrists, clinical social workers, marriage and family therapists, and mental health counselors. While each of these disciplines or specialties has unique skills, each has many skills in common with those possessed by the clinical psychologist. Since admission and graduation requirements are different, some of the other types of professionals, such as social workers and mental health counselors, may be able to offer a potential employer most, if not all, of the same skills that could be offered by the clinical psychologist, and they can provide other benefits to the employer as well (such as being willing to work for a lower salary).

It has long been recognized that mental health professionals, especially when they are performing therapeutic services, have more similarities than differences. Fiedler (1950) found that therapists of various theoretical schools of therapy did not differ in their descriptions of the concepts for an ideal therapeutic relationship (their degree of expertise, not their theoretical allegiance, was thought to be the significant factor). Strupp (1955) compared the psychotherapeutic techniques of psychiatrists, psychologists, and psychiatric social workers, and concluded that the disciplinary affiliation exerted, at the most, was only a relatively minor influence (when theoretical orientation was held constant).

CLINICAL PSYCHOLOGY VERSUS COUNSELING PSYCHOLOGY AND SCHOOL PSYCHOLOGY

Clinical psychology has always been closely akin to counseling psychology and school psychology. From its early days, clinical psychology was believed to emphasize psychopathology, whereas counseling psychology was believed to emphasize normality or hygiology—the condition of health or absence of clinically defined illness (Super, 1955). The training programs in the two specialties were and are highly similar in content, except perhaps for the site of the internship and a difference in the amount of coursework in abnormal behavior (i.e., more for clinical psychology) and vocational development (i.e., more for counseling psychology). The eminent clinical psychology trainer at Purdue University, the late John M. Hadley (1961), chose to consider clinical and counseling psychology together, which seemed to be the harbinger of the contemporary "professional psychology" stance of many psychologists in health care. School psychology received much of its impetus from clinical psychologists who had an interest in serving children. The schools afforded an access route, and some training programs have joined clinical psychology and school psychology together (Vane, 1985). Furthermore, Lightner Witmer, considered to be a "founding father" of both clinical and school psychology, worked with educationally related problems.

As for employment, Tipton (1983) studied the roles and functions that could distinguish clinical psychologists from counseling psychologists. He found the normality (or hygiology) to pathology continuum, with the counseling psychologists being—as Super (1955) posited four decades ago—more aligned with normality, and clinical psychologists more aligned with pathology. There were, however, many similarities, but: (1) clinical psychologists maintained an assessment–diagnostic component, with minimal reference to therapy for a relatively normal population; (2) clinical psychologists gave more support than counseling psychologists to providing marital interventions and other consultations; and (3) "Particularly notable among the discrepancies between how the specialties rated the relevance of the activities for counseling psychology were the following four activities that were given significantly lower ratings by the clinical group: counseling/therapy with adults, counseling/therapy with the mild to moderately disturbed, preventative treatment, and outreach programs" (Tipton, 1983, p. 844).

In the 1990s, there seems to be a blending, such as by state licensing laws, of the specialties of clinical, counseling, and school psychology. Also, the contexts in which psychological services are being provided accept the blending of the specialties. Clinical services in the schools, reflecting a continuing unity of clinical and school psychology, are receiving public and professional support (Murray, 1995). Further, with families being served in a more comprehensive (and clinical) fashion by schools, there is greater collaboration between clinical, counseling, and school psychologists (Christenson, 1995). Rather than the formal name of the training program from which the psychologist graduated determining his or her specialty identification, the particular service context or idiosyncratic competencies and proficiencies of the psychologist serve as the primary determinants.

CLINICAL PSYCHOLOGY VERSUS PSYCHIATRY

Even though the psychiatrist may treat pathological patients, he or she is not qualified to administer and interpret psychological tests. Of course, the clinical psychologist is not, to this date, qualified to prescribe medication, and this provides for a logical teamwork effort for the clinical psychologist and the psychiatrist. It must be recognized, however, that clinical psychologists are, in fact, starting to become trained in psychopharmacology and prescription of medications, and it seems probable that at least limited prescription privileges will be granted by federal and state governmental sources in the foreseeable future.

It is a reality that clinical psychologists have more extensive training and greater depth to their understanding of normal and abnormal human behavior than representatives from certain other disciplines. More extensive training is particularly manifest in research methods and psychotherapy such as comparative analyses; these combine to produce a clear-cut scientific basis for the practice of psychology, something that may or may not be present in psychiatric training. Rather than denigrating another discipline (such as psychiatry), the best strategy is to sell the qualifications of the clinical psychologist for expertise. There has been far too much warring among mental health professionals for what can only be deemed ego gratification or enhancement of income, and which can be interpreted only as being fueled by a faulty professional self-identity and objectives.

Clinical psychology has matured to the point where it is in no way second to any other profession or discipline. Clinical psychology need not be in "competition" with other psychological specialties, such as counseling psychology and school psychology, or with psychiatry, social work, or mental health counseling. Each specialty or discipline has its unique proficiencies to offer to the health care system and society.

SPECIALIZED CREDENTIALS

In keeping with the earlier comments about specialty guidelines, obtaining employment as a clinical psychologist is increasingly reliant upon skills that will separate one applicant from another applicant. In other words, it is recognized that clinical psychology is a complex specialty, one that includes so many possible areas of expertise that it is impossible for every clinical psychologist to possess equal competence in each of them. Consequently, specialized credentials have been developed (and more are assuredly on the way) that will provide distinction.

Today, there is a proliferation of specialty credentials, and while this presumably helps safeguard standards for the consumer, it is not without problems. As President of the APA's Division of Clinical Psychology, Lee B. Sechrest

(1985) states: "Psychology, and clinical psychology which is at the crux of the matter, appears to be headed toward the creation of 'specialties' at a frightful rate"; and he notes that "there are now about 30 (!) different groups proposing themselves as specialties" (p. 1). While acknowledging the "to protect the public" rationale, Sechrest critically asserts that there are two other motives: (1) specialty diplomas accommodate advertising that will increase income; for example, "Specialists expect to charge higher fees, and the evidence from medicine is certainly that they do" (p. 1); and (2):

> One suspects also that just sheer ego has something to do with the problem of specialization. Most diplomas, at least in psychology, are probably of very little material value; they may serve no greater purpose than persuading their possessors that they are in some way special. Presumably some warm feeling flows through the practitioner who can gaze upon the large array of neatly framed documents decorating his or her office wall. One of my colleagues has suggested that we go into business manufacturing diploma wallpaper that could simplify the whole thing [p. 1].

Although it may sound as though Sechrest is a heretic regarding his clinical psychology specialty, such is not the case. He goes on to encourage assembling evidence to support standards, arrangements, and a specialty that will "truly protect the public and preserve that honorable practice of psychology" (p. 3).

DIPLOMATING BOARDS

There are, of course, some boards that award specialty diplomas that are worth little more than a "buy your diploma" operation, and nothing good can be said for those boards that are in business to collect application fees and award (read "sell") the diploma simply for payment.

There are, however, two other types of specialty diploma boards that are more legitimate. The first type has several members of the board review that applicant's credentials, and those candidates receiving endorsement are given the diploma without an examination. The second type of board requires a credential review, a work sample for analysis, and an examination. This approach is certainly an honorable peer-review process, which contributes positively to upgrading the profession.

As noted in the Sechrest comments, there are many specialty boards, and it would be inappropriate to try to list them all or pass judgment on them. Suffice it to say, a specialty credential is possible in behavioral medicine, biofeedback, hypnosis, psychotherapy, marriage and sex therapy, child custody, and administrative, vocational, forensic, and family psychology, and so on.

THE AMERICAN BOARD
OF PROFESSIONAL PSYCHOLOGY

The American Board of Professional Psychology (ABPP) was founded in 1947. As of 1994, there were 3313 living diplomates, of whom 881 were retired; and of the total number, there were 2023 living diplomates in clinical psychology, of whom 566 were retired (American Board of Professional Psychology, personal communication, 1994).

In brief, the "Purposes and Aims" of the ABPP are:

(1) to arrange and conduct investigations and examinations to determine the qualifications of individuals who apply for the Diplomas issued by the Corporation; (2) to award such Diplomas in the field of professional psychology to qualified applicants therefore (sic), and to maintain a registry of holders of such Diplomas; (3) to serve the public welfare by preparing and furnishing to proper persons and agencies lists of specialists who have been awarded Diplomas by the Corporation; and (4) to serve

the public welfare by undertaking or sponsoring programs designed to enhance the quality of professional
service. . . . The Board encourages the pursuit of excellence via its program of certification at an advanced
professional level. The ABPP Diploma signifies, to the
public and to the profession, the highest recognition of
competence as judged by one's professional peers [Ameri-
can Board of Professional Psychology, 1994, p. 1].

The ABPP conducts a demanding examination program.
To be an approved candidate, a psychologist must have
high-quality training (there are specific conditions that
must be fulfilled by the candidate's doctoral program) and
experience. Among other experience factors, there must
be an internship, plus four years of acceptable qualifying
experience, with three of those years being postdoctoral.
If approved to move forward in the examination process,
the candidate can submit work samples for peer review,
and if they pass muster, move on to the formal examination. The latter can vary somewhat, but typically includes
working with an actual patient while being observed
through a one-way window by several examiners. Work
samples may be used in an oral examination format.
    Successful completion of the examination leads
to award of diplomate status. In 1995, one can become
diplomated in nine areas. The specialties and the number
of Diplomates in each are: clinical psychology (2004); school
psychology (310); counseling psychology (299); clinical
neuropsychology (241); forensic psychology (about 150);
industrial/organizational psychology (about 150); family
psychology (94); behavioral psychology (46); and health
psychology (25). In 1996, group psychology was added as a
specialty (American Board of Professional Psychology,
1996). Reportedly, psychoanalysis and rehabilitation psychology, and possibly assessment psychology may be added
in the future (Academy of Clinical Psychology, 1995). It
should be noted that the areas of family, behavioral, and
health were added recently, and their lesser numbers should

not be interpreted as an indication of any market potential. As evident from the numbers presented in the preceding paragraph, the large majority of diplomas awarded by ABPP are in the specialty of clinical psychology. A psychologist can become a diplomate in more than one specialty, but only if an examination is successfully completed for each specialization. For example (and as was the case with the senior author of this book), a clinical psychologist might initially become a diplomate in clinical psychology, reflecting his or her overall professional identity and competency, but because of additional training and involvement in legal cases (e.g., giving expert testimony), he or she could potentially also become a diplomate in forensic psychology. Any combination of the nine specialties is possible.

The APA, while independent of the ABPP, recognizes the diplomates created by ABPP and its affiliates, as well as those psychologists who have been named diplomates of psychological hypnosis by the American Board of Psychological Hypnosis (ABPH). This recognition is somewhat nominal, but the aforementioned diplomates are listed in the APA's membership directory, and the diplomate status from these sources is sometimes listed in the directories of state-level psychological associations. To date, the APA has not granted recognition, even in a nominal manner, to any of the many other independent (non-ABPP) specialty boards.

Among psychologists, holding ABPP diplomate status is an honor. It signifies that the psychologist's credentials have been inspected and approved by peers; his or her work product has been scrutinized and endorsed as supporting the potential for effectiveness; and he or she has satisfied the standards of a professional examination that is both academic and clinical in nature. Stated succinctly, the ABPP diplomate is deemed to be an exceptional clinical psychologist by the profession. Nietzel, Bernstein, and Milich (1994) state: "An ABPP diploma is considered more prestigious than licensure, although it carries no legal authority" (p. 453).

The nature of the ABPP diplomating process and the high qualities of the diplomates has led to legal recognition, however. In some states, the laws and rules pertaining to licensing allow certain exceptions for persons holding ABPP diplomate status. It is commonplace for certain employment positions, particularly those at a more senior level, to specify that applicants should hold the ABPP diploma. In addition, an ABPP diplomate might also justify a higher salary or fee for service. For example, Senator Daniel K. Inouye (1984) spearheaded the passage of the Veterans Health Care and Facilities Improvement Act of 1984, which was ratified by the 98th Congress, and provided authority to give a pay bonus of up to $10,000 for those clinical or counseling psychologists who were ABPP diplomates.

PROFESSIONAL MEMBERSHIP

A clinical psychologist's claim to specialization can also gain credence through membership in certain professional organizations. There are some professional organizations that admit virtually any professional who pays the dues and which may provide a handsome certificate to display on the office wall. This type of membership does little, if anything, to document training, competency, or expertise. On the other hand, there are certain other professional organizations which have stringent requirements for membership; that is, being a psychologist, expressing interest, filling out an application form, and paying the dues are not enough to gain membership.

When membership in a professional organization is restricted to those who can document having had, as a minimum, specialized coursework and supervised experience, it seems reasonable to deem the membership to be a form of certification of competency, albeit less rigorous and less esteemed than having obtained certification through a peer-administered examination process. Some organizations of this type go beyond coursework, such as in psychotherapy, having personally received some therapeutic or psychological growth experience that would presumably equip the psychologist with insight about his or her personal–professional self-concept (as might be critical to the competency needed later on to deal with transference–countertransference issues); in group psychotherapy, having conducted a certain number of therapy groups of a particular duration; or in sex therapy, having treated a certain number of patients with sexual problems.

In most of these specialties, it is common also to require a certain amount of clinical supervision of one's services, with the supervision being provided by a more senior professional in the specialty. For example, the American Association for Marriage and Family Therapy (AAMFT), which predicates clinical member status on a number of qualifications, requires that (unless an individual qualifies for a "hardship" exception) some of the supervision be provided by an approved supervisor, a marriage and family therapist previously approved by the organization for its roster of supervisors.

As with the ABPP diplomate status, it is not unusual for an announcement of a position in, say, marriage and family therapy, to specify that preference is for a psychologist who is, for example, a clinical member of the AAMFT, or if the position is in training, such as with a university, to prefer an AAMFT approved supervisor. If the position involves conducting group psychotherapy, it would be a plus (if not a prerequisite) to be a member of the American Group Psychotherapy Association (AGPA), since it specifies a number of qualities relevant to training and experience before membership is granted.

Although not a certification of competency per se, achieving fellow status within a professional organization can complement employment potential. By being active in, say, the committee work of a professional organization and becoming an elected officer, or in some other manner making a distinguished contribution, a psychologist can become a fellow. Being named a Fellow of the APA would be an asset in the job market; it would signify that the individual had made an outstanding contribution to his or her professional discipline.

SPECIALIZED TRAINING EXPERIENCES

Distinctive training in a specialization can be a noteworthy credential. For example, having one's doctoral internship in a unique context, say a neuropsychology facility, would afford a benefit when a position involving neuropsychology was sought. Grace (1985) offers guidelines for evaluating prospective clinical internships.

Many clinical psychologists do a postdoctoral fellowship in order to gain advanced specialization. Indeed, postdoctoral training has become so common, one recent university search committee found that every applicant for a lower-level professorship had completed a postdoctoral training experience. Note, however, that applicants applying for university employment would be more apt to have formal postdoctoral training than, say, those applying for employment in a community mental health center or as an associate in a private practice group.

On a more modest level, completion of continuing education seminars, which is consonant with the ethical responsibility for every psychologist, can serve to form a specialization. If this informal or unsystematic approach is chosen, the clinical psychologist will likely have to rely on his or her power of persuasion to convince potential employers of the quality of the self-determined specialization.

It should be noted that certain continuing education experiences will be better than others for this purpose. For example, there have been a number of training programs in hypnosis that could actually taint a professional's reputation (e.g., the training was conducted by laypersons with a "stage hypnotism" flare), whereas training in hypnosis from a reputable source could be an important aid in seeking a position in, say, a health psychology context.

EMPLOYMENT OPPORTUNITIES AND INCOME

It should be emphasized that the political and economic conditions of the 1990s have resulted in a tight job market for clinical psychologists. As discussed earlier, the public policy press for accountability and cost containment by health care providers and the diminution of public tax-based support of mental health programs, along with the emergence of managed health care from the corporate sector, paint an employment picture that is much different from what could be viewed in previous decades.

By the beginning of the twenty-first century, the marketplace could, however, have changed considerably from its situation in the 1990s. Earlier, it was emphasized that the current public policy state of affairs should not be considered to constitute an irreparable or unmalleable employment market for clinical psychologists. Realistic appraisal of the existing conditions can be used to reframe the situation to being a challenge to trigger a rigorous pursuit of excellence, which can result in expanded service and employment opportunities for clinical psychologists.

Some of the shrinkage of job opportunities is due to the large number of psychologists that have been trained. For example, from 1966 to 1976, there was a 153 percent increase in the number of psychology doctorates awarded (Syverson, 1982). In recent years, however, the number of advanced degrees in psychology awarded has resulted in only a moderate increase (National Science Foundation, 1988).

The sheer number of candidates vying for certain clinical jobs means that, no matter what the applicant's qualifications, the prospect of being selected is relatively minimal. Due to the proficiencies of professionals trained in other disciplines (e.g., social work and mental health counseling), the greatest competition seems to be for positions that involve therapeutic services.

On the other hand, training in clinical psychology provides exceptional qualifications (e.g., for medical and forensic services). Also, an array of nontraditional employment settings welcome clinical psychologists, such as correctional facilities, industries, government agencies, and schools. Given the current governmental priority for assigning responsibilities relevant to social, behavioral, and health problems in children and youth to school-based personnel, the job market for clinical psychologists with adequate concomitant training in education is strong within school systems.

Since the present job market for clinical psychologists is difficult at best, it will be the exception rather than the rule to be able to target a particular type of employment, select a desired geographical locale, readily obtain a job there, work in it for a while, and then move eventually to a position that will represent an advancement. Steinhauser (1985) discusses his experiences when seeking employment as a new Ph.D. holder. Even though he recognized before he started that the job market was crowded, that he could not restrict himself to a dream job, and that he could not choose a geographical location, he made 122 job applications, had 10 interviews, and received two job offers. Today, the same ratio (or worse) exists.

The message, therefore, is that obtaining employment is a challenge. It requires cultivating professional and personal qualities. The candidate must earn academic credentials that will be equal to or greater than those possessed by other candidates. Personally, the candidate must not place his or her ego in jeopardy by expecting immediate employment. It is not a sign of failure to be denied a job in this day and age, it is merely the product of a complex array of political, financial, and social factors.

Since 1975, the APA has assessed the employment status of those with new psychology doctorates. In her employment survey of psychology graduates with master's, specialist's, and related degrees (i.e., subdoctoral degrees), Gehlmann (1994) found that: "56% were employed full time, 12% were employed part time, 11% were employed but did not indicate whether their employment was full time or part time, 3% were enrolled in a doctoral program, 6% were unemployed and seeking, 8% were unemployed and not seeking, 3% indicated some other type of employment status, and 1% did not specify" (unnumbered). As for the employment scene, "Forty percent of the respondents said the job market was fair, while 30% said that it was good" (unnumbered). As for incomes, the highest median salaries (converted to 11–12 month periods) were "reported by those in applied psychology settings ($42,000) and school psychology human service settings ($38,000)"; and she concludes, "Overall, those in school psychology and applied psychology positions were paid higher salaries than those in clinical and counseling positions" (unnumbered).

In a survey of employment of doctoral level psychologists, Kohout and Wicherski (1991) noted an increase in the number of Psy.D. degrees over the last decade (12% of new doctorates in psychology), and report: "Over three fourths of the new doctorates were employed full time (78%), a tenth (10%) were employed part time, 9% were postdoctoral fellows and less than 2% indicated that they were unemployed and seeking employment" (p. 3). As for employment setting:

> The primary settings for full-time employed doctorate recipients were hospitals (20%), university settings (17%), and business, government and other (13%). Approximately 10% each were employed in independent practice, clinics and other human service settings (e.g., university/college counseling center, special services such as for mentally handicapped and aged) and nursing homes. Eight percent

were located in schools and other educational settings,
while about 4%, each, were employed in four-year college
settings and medical schools. Less than 2% were found in
other academic settings such as two-year colleges or professional schools [p. 5].

They note that from 1981 to 1989, "the top three settings
remained the same but the ordering had changed slightly
to hospitals, university settings, business, government,
and other" (p. 5).

Salaries are always of interest. The following sources
are illustrative, but there will always be other factors that
must be considered before formulating any notion about
what salary is deserved or possible. Under the auspices of
the APA, Kohout and Wicherski (1991) conducted a survey
of recipients of doctoral degrees in psychology between July
1, 1988, and June 30, 1989. The following mean incomes
were revealed (based on all settings for each category):
Assistant Professor, $30,014; Research Positions, $37,000;
Direct Human Services—Clinical Psychology, $39,610; Di-
rect Human Services—Counseling Psychology, $35,900;
Direct Human Services—School Psychology, $44,400; Ad-
ministration of Human Services, $40,480; and Other Ap-
plied Psychology, $45,470. The mean income for clinical
psychologists in "Individual Private Practice" was $51,980
and "Group Psychological Practice" was $45,820.

Gehlmann (1994) conducted a similar APA survey of
recipients of master's, specialist's, and related degrees in
psychology between July 1, 1991, and June 30, 1992. Note
that while some doctoral psychologists were included, the
data from this survey are not restricted to doctoral level psychologists, as was true in the Kohout and Wicherski (1991)
survey discussed in the preceding paragraph. Gehlmann
reports the following mean incomes (based on all settings
for each category): Research Positions, $29,235; Direct
Human Services—Clinical Psychology, $24,145; Direct
Human Services—Counseling Psychology, $27,800;
Direct Human Services—School Psychology, $36,446;

Administration of Human Services, $33,380; and Other Applied Psychology, $37,144. The median income (no mean income was reported) for clinical psychologists in "Private and Group Practice" was $24,000.

When comparing the respondents in the two surveys under the auspices of APA (Kohout and Wicherski, 1991; Gehlmann, 1994), it is apparent that the three-year span led to a decrease in every category. However, as was noted, the respondents in the Gehlmann survey were not all at the doctoral level, and thus any attempted comparison is likely to involve "mixing apples and oranges." Nonetheless, a decrease in incomes (and, indeed, the training level of certain types of health care providers, such as mental health therapists) is, of course, in keeping with comments made throughout this book about emphasis on cost reduction imposed by this health care reform era, as well as the national societal trend for incomes to decrease in virtually all areas of employment. Recall, as mentioned earlier, however, that Fowler (1995) believes that psychologists have experienced increases in incomes above the cost of living.

Being a specialist commonly increases income. In a survey of neuropsychologists, Putnam and Anderson (1994) noted a 7 percent increase in salaries since 1988, and report "a median income of $76,022 and a mean income of $95,955 for 1992" (p. 3). In a salary survey of ABPP counseling psychology diplomates (of whom many likely had a clinical background), Talley (1990) indicates: "The highest mean salary ($68,400) was earned by those with 6–10 years experience; the lowest ($54,472) was earned by those with 11–15 years experience. All other levels of experience had mean salary levels between these two figures" (p. 504).

As for private practice of clinical psychology, surveys generally suggest that the income is relatively high. While the two employment surveys under the auspices of APA (Kohout and Wicherski, 1991; Gehlmann, 1994) might be interpreted as reflecting a decrease in clinical psychologists'

incomes, the economic volatility of the private practice sector potentially fosters misinformation. Suffice it to say, most
pundits likely believe that incomes from private practice of
clinical psychology are not increasing at the moment and
are, at best, impossible to predict in the future.

The incomes of psychology professors deserve special
consideration. *The Chronicle of Higher Education* (1994)
reports that the average psychology faculty salaries at
public four-year institutions in 1993–1994 were: instruc-
tor, $28,525; new assistant professor, $33,013; assistant
professor (including new assistant professors), $34,817;
associate professor, $43,649; professor, $56,259; and all
ranks, $46,546. In an APA survey of faculty salaries in
doctoral programs in psychology in 1994–1995, the average salaries were: lecturer/instructor, $37,254; assistant
professor, $39,147; associate professor, $47,539; full professor, $66,682; and all ranks, $55,193 (Wicherski and
Kohout, 1995). Fowler (1995) states:

> Many members believe that applied psychologists make
> more than faculty members, but data from our income
> surveys indicate that the income differential between
> practitioners and academics is quite small. Psychologists
> teaching in departments with doctoral programs have a
> median salary of $57,600 for 9 to 10 months. Practitio-
> ners in health-service-delivery settings have a median
> income of $60,000 for 12 months. The increase in academic
> salaries over the past 10 years has been 54 percent and
> the increase for practitioners has been 50 percent [p. 3].

Subsequently, Wicherski and Kohout (1996) provides a
follow-up analysis of 1995–1996 faculty salaries.

CONTINUING EDUCATION

Employment will be influenced by the strong trend toward
specialization, which, among other things, has created the
responsibility of clinical psychologists to maintain, enhance, or retool their skills. Continuing education (CE)

started coming on strong during the late 1970s in response to several concerns.

In clinical psychology, new knowledge is always needed. Aside from professionalism per se, the press for increasing knowledge and skills is part of the demand for accountability by the public, government regulatory agencies, private third-party reimbursers, legislatures and consumer groups (Kalafat and Neigher, 1983). Also, serious questions remain about the adequacy and relevancy of traditional graduate training in psychology (Karon, 1995a). Some solutions and answers will presumably come from continuing education.

There is a definite trend among states to require CE credits for relicensure, namely for the purpose of proving that the licensee is making a reasonable effort to maintain professional competencies and develop skills to enhance service to consumers. To assure optimum employability, clinical psychologists must maintain a commitment to continuing education throughout their career.

EMPLOYMENT PROGNOSIS

Considerable comment has already been made about how predicting employment opportunities can only be highly speculative. There are always too many unknown and unpredictable conditions that can alter the employment trend to allow for confident or assured predictions. This inability to knowingly predict was certainly witnessed over the past three decades. Given the surge of public policy support for mental health in the 1960s, the allocation of governmental funding to develop training programs, and the proliferation of graduates in psychology, few soothsayers would or could have predicted the radical shift away from human services, and the concomitant underemployment and unemployment of clinical psychologists that has occurred.

For now, it can be said that there is likely to be a continuing decline in employment in certain settings, such as colleges and universities, but there will likely be an increase in employment in other settings, such as in legal, educational, medical, and hospital settings (Mozdzierz, Snodgrass, and DeLeon, 1992; Matarazzo, 1992; Enright, Resnick, Ludwigsen, and DeLeon, 1993; DeAngelis, 1994).

It seems likely that the private practice of clinical psychology will become even more widely accepted and relied upon by the public and will, therefore, create new employment possibilities, albeit health care will be controlled by governmental and third-party (e.g., insurance and managed health care) sources. Since there has been unbridled training of practitioners in other mental health disciplines (e.g., psychiatry, social work, and mental health counseling) and given the diminution of governmental support for mental health services, it is incontrovertible that there is an abundance of private practitioners for mental health services. While many of these practitioners are not as well qualified as clinical psychologists, their availability and the public policy press to achieve cost reduction for health care services make private practice more competitive and less lucrative than in the 1980s. Consequently, clinical psychologists will likely move toward other settings or contexts.

Public policy supports the private practice of clinical psychology, but there is a push to place clinical psychologists, along with other health care providers, under a national health care plan. The economic domination that accompanies a national health care plan and commercial managed health care corporations threatens professional autonomy. While it is impossible to knowledgeably forecast the effects of the health care reform movement, it is feasible that it could either enhance or undermine the practice of clinical psychology.

Having issued cautions, a note of optimism is in order. It seems that clinical psychology has developed in a professionally unprecedented manner. From modest roots at the turn of the century, it has blossomed into a mature health care discipline that is nourished by an impeccable, scientifically derived energy. Public policy has acknowledged this stature, and recognized that clinical psychology has accomplished much good for society.

Among all of the psychological specialties, clinical psychology seems to have one of the most solid curricular frameworks for its graduates. Consequently, the clinical psychologist, in keeping with the scientist–practitioner model, is capable of changing with the times. Few of the other psychological specialties can boast of the generalizability of academic foundations and the adaptability of practice competencies of clinical psychology.

The endorsement by public policy and the scientist–practitioner composition generate optimism about the employment potential of the clinical psychologist. Stated differently, even if there are rough spots in the employment road ahead for psychologists (e.g., due to the health care reform movement), clinical psychologists (as compared to members of other mental health specialties or disciplines) are apt to have a relatively smooth passage.

Chapter 7

Being Professional: Ethics And Law

"You know," said the clinical psychologist, "I was taught by my professors that I should advocate the interests of my clients according to social ideals and follow the APA ethics to the letter. I have been doing therapy with two children who live with their mother, and her ex-spouse, the kids' father, keeps badgering her, taking her to court over every little thing. He has really made life miserable for them all. She does not want me to give him any information about what she or the children tell me, and he demanded a copy of the records for the children. I refused him, thinking I was advocating the interests of my client, and the next thing that I knew, I received a complaint from the state licensing board, alleging that I was in violation of the board's rules. I have just received a subpoena from the father's attorney demanding that I appear for a deposition next week, apparently to bring all of my records and talk about the treatment that I have been providing to the mother, as well as the children. I know the father just intends to use what I say against the mother in court. I did exactly what I thought ethics required and certainly acted the way my professors urged, and now I have to hire an attorney to defend me before my own licensing board, and take time away from seeing other clients to give the deposition. Somebody is wrong and the legal system is certainly screwed up!"

More will be said about this scenario as this chapter explores how the field of clinical psychology is now regulated by nonpsychological sources.

INTRODUCTION

In considering the regulation of clinical psychology, it could be asserted that clinical psychologists should have the prerogative of relying on self-determination for their professional functioning. After all, every clinical psychologist has survived countless challenges in graduate school and has proven to a distinguished faculty of clinical psychology trainers that he or she merits wearing the mantle of professionalism—otherwise, the doctoral degree would not have been awarded.

Typically, a clinical psychologist has also been subjected to extensive evaluation on the postdoctoral level, such as through taking a national standardized (objective) examination, writing a state-ordered essay, or an oral examination, in order to obtain licensure to practice psychology. Of course, as noted, many clinical psychologists voluntarily subject themselves to additional evaluations, such as seeking diplomate status from the American Board of Professional Psychology (ABPP).

The rationale for self-determination would be that since the clinical psychologist has successfully passed so many assessments, it would seem reasonable to allow autonomous decision making about professional practices. After all, no other source is better able to judge what is needed by the client than the professional with firsthand contacts. For the skeptic of autonomous decision making, there would be the alternative of letting clinical psychologists, as a group, regulate themselves. That is, given the uniqueness of clinical psychology, only clinical psychologists would have the knowledge necessary for establishing professional practices. This would be termed the *peer review* approach.

As logical as these two alternatives might seem, neither prevails today. There is, of course, a large amount of autonomous decision making virtually every moment in the practice of clinical psychology, and peer review still fulfills an important role, but there are other sources of control and regulation. In this day and age, there are many decisions made about the practice of clinical psychology by sources that are nonpsychological in nature, and which are vested by society with legal authority to make these decisions and enforce compliance by practicing psychologists.

Regulatory sources can be, therefore, either psychological or nonpsychological. Most often, psychologists assume that psychological considerations are the exclusive determinants of standards, but as will emerge, there are other considerations, not the least of which are economic.

According to Claiborn (1982), there are seven organizational contexts that constitute primary means for ensuring competence in professional psychology: standards for providers; ethical codes; professional standards review committees; third-party payer quality assurance; state licensing and certification boards; the National Register; and diplomate status. What deserves emphasis, however, is that these seven sources acknowledged by Claiborn fail to include the controlling regulation that has emerged from legislative and common law and managed health care.

NONPSYCHOLOGICAL REGULATORS

Before exploring the different sources that have regulatory impact on the practice of clinical psychology, consideration should be given to why authority to oversee psychological practices has been given to nonpsychological sources. As will be obvious, the reason does not speak well for professionalism.

At one time, society supported that a profession could and should regulate itself. The learned professions, especially those with a scientific thrust (like psychology), were accepted by society as being in the best position to determine standards and judge the propriety of the conduct of

its members. The underlying premise was "more depend-
able knowledge is attained through science because science ultimately appeals to evidence: propositions are
subjected to empirical test" (Kerlinger, 1964, p. 8). This
principle supported that a professional discipline would
have views about what was justified scientifically in practice, and would enforce the standards to keep errant practitioners out of the profession. Etzioni (1969) championed
professional autonomy, saying, "Only if immune from or-
dinary social pressures and free to innovate, to experiment,
to take risks without the usual social repercussions of failure, can a professional carry out his work effectively . . ."
(p. x). Consequently, in the 1960s and part of the 1970s,
any regulation of psychological practice came essentially
from the American Psychological Association (APA), and
any disciplinary action against an allegedly errant psychologist was implemented by an ethics committee, be it
at the national, state, or local level. By the mid-1970s,
however, this exclusive regulatory role began to erode and
dwindle in its quasi-authority.

In the past two decades, society has become skeptical about virtually all professional services, especially
those in the realm of health care. Believing that societal
problems are complex and idealism is dead, Fein (1981)
pointed out that, "The call is for hard heads, not soft
hearts, and, in the view of many, these are mutually exclusive organs of the body politic" (p. 32).

The 1960s allowed an abundance of professional opportunity, freedom from regulation, and funding for health
care (including mental health) services. Some practitioners
demonstrated greedy opportunism and abused the health
care system. The professional associations failed to achieve
strict enforcement of standards or to adequately protect
the public via ethics committees. This did not go unno-
ticed. Bice (1981) refers to the 1960s as a "watershed"
period for health services, and the unacceptable self-
regulation by professional associations resulted in a

societal call for more governmental and legal regulation in the 1970s.

Perhaps the turning point for the mental health professions, including psychology, was when the courthouse doors were thrown open to allow mental health practitioners to be sued for failing to protect society from dangerous and violent clients, as per the well-known 1976 *Tarasoff* case (VandeCreek and Knapp, 1993). At about the same time, various legal cases produced judgments that held mental health practitioners accountable for their conduct in ways that had never before been enforced.

Also in the 1970s, state licensing boards began to proliferate, promulgating legal rules. This amounted to a macrolevel setting of standards for micropractice. Further, the legislation and concomitant rules relevant to licensing psychologists were often written or strongly influenced (some psychologists would likely say "dictated") by the attorneys who advised the licensing boards. It is somewhat ironic that many psychologists pushed licensing, thinking it would enhance their status and incomes, when the result was actually less self-determination and more governmental and legal regulation of psychological practices. Now in this era of commercialized managed health care and health care reform, governmental control is spearheading cost containment, which may mean less income for clinical psychologists.

As third-party payment sources (e.g., insurance companies) increased the coverage of mental health treatments, abuses (e.g., fraudulent billings) and higher fees (i.e., if the client had insurance) caused the public, the insurance industry, and government lawmakers to be disenchanted with mental health practitioners. Cost containment became the byword. Concerned about rising costs for the health insurance that they provided to their employees, employers embraced managed health care, such as employee assistance programs (EAPs) and health maintenance organizations (HMOs).

All the while, malpractice law suits against mental health professionals continued to increase (Besharov, 1985; Fisher, 1985). In the minds of the public policy makers, mental health practice had become an industry; it was no longer a benevolent human service that deserved special dispensation or immunity from legal liability.

What this regulatory evolution actually reflects is that the professional self-regulation that was accommodated by society in the past had failed. All too often, professional self-regulation had seemed to benefit the profession (via an "Old Boys/Girls Club" mentality) at the expense of society (i.e., failure to either compensate clients damaged by errant practitioners or protect other clients from similar negligence or wrongful conduct in the future). There is ample reason to assert that the failure of self-regulation contributed mightily to the health care reform movement, with its diminution of professional status and demand for accountability and cost containment (actually, cost reduction) (Starr, 1994).

HISTORICAL STANDARDS

For clinical psychologists, the standards prepared by the APA are, with the exception of any overriding standards set forth by law (as will be discussed later), of foremost importance. However, the APA standards are constantly changing, and nothing herein should be interpreted as being cast in cement.

Historically and as mentioned earlier in this book, an important document came from the APA Committee on Professional Standards (APA, 1981), and provided "specialty guidelines" for clinical psychology, counseling psychology, industrial–organizational psychology, and school psychology. Later, "General Guidelines for Providers of Psychological Services" (APA, 1987b) were also promulgated. Since the purpose of this discussion is historical illustration (and modern-day standards will be detailed later), coverage in this section will be restricted to the specialty guidelines for clinical psychology (hereinafter referred to as the "1981 specialty guidelines"). It should be noted that these specialty guidelines are still useful for clarifying the nature of standards, but no longer deserve to be considered the prevailing standards. The 1981 specialty guidelines are, however, discussed here to show how a professional organization, to wit the APA, began its movement toward the specific standards that are in effect today.

The primary purpose of the 1981 specialty guidelines was to promote the best interests and welfare of the consumer of the clinical psychologist's services (note that the guidelines referred to the clinical psychologist as the "provider" and the patient or recipient of services as the "user"). The intention was to provide assurance that the clinical psychologist would be accountable for the nature and quality of services (but not to the point that new methods or innovative procedures would be negated).

The specialty guidelines sought to: (1) "provide a foundation for mutual understanding between provider and user and facilitate more effective evaluation of services provided and outcomes achieved" (p. 641); (2) foster uniformity for the credentialing of clinical psychologists; (3) "give specific content to the profession's concept of ethical practice as it applies to the functions of clinical psychologists" (p. 641); (4) have an impact on future education and training models for clinical psychologists (and their support personnel); (5) "influence the determination of acceptable structure, budgeting, and staffing patterns" (p. 641) in the health service facilities that employ clinical psychologists; and (6) obtain continual review and revision of the guidelines applied to clinical psychology. Thus, the specialty guidelines were developed to improve the quality and delivery of clinical psychological services: "Systematically applied, these Guidelines serve to establish a more effective and consistent basis for evaluating the performance of individual service providers as well as to guide the organization of clinical psychological service units in human service settings" (p. 641).

Guideline 1: Providers, specified standards for: (1) establishing the availability of clinical psychologists within a service unit; (2) supervising minimally qualified providers; (3) involving a clinical psychologist in planning, directing, and reviewing services; (4) influencing overall organizational goals, planning, and development; (5) maintaining up-to-date knowledge of scientific and professional developments; (6) limiting practice to areas of demonstrated competence; (7) having consonance between practice and education-training standards; and (8) encouraging innovative theories and procedures.

Guideline 2: Programs, dealt with the composition and organization of clinical psychological services, such as: (1) being responsive to the needs of persons or settings served; (2) delineating lines of responsibility (including for supervision and accountability); (3) having sufficient numbers of professional and support personnel; (4) protecting the legal and civil rights of users; (5) adhering to standards and ethical principles promulgated by the APA; (6) conforming to statutory laws; (7) being informed about and linked to the community network of human services; (8) maintaining collegiality to meet the best interests of users; and (9) having proper procedural guidelines within the service unit for the delivery of clinical psychological services (e.g., effective records, a system for confidentiality).

Guideline 3: Accountability, was devoted to promoting human welfare, and held that: "Clinical psychologists pursue their activities as members of the independent autonomous profession of psychology" (p. 647); that is, no other profession or discipline could govern the profession of psychology. The latter, while not stated per se, supported that clinical psychology should not be subservient to another discipline, such as medicine, and any service unit that created conditions for employment that would require such subservience was unacceptable to the standards of clinical psychology. This guideline also promoted "periodic, systematic, and effective evaluations of clinical psychological services" (p. 648).

Guideline 4: Environment, set forth the promotion of facilitative physical, organizational, and social environments for the unit offering clinical psychological services. This included meeting legal requirements for safety, health, and sanitation, and being concerned about any condition that could potentially have an adverse effect on the quality of services; for example, "Physical arrangements and organizational policies and procedures are conducive to the human dignity, self-respect, and optimal functioning of users and to the effective delivery of service" (p. 648).

From this synopsis of the 1981 specialty guidelines, it is evident that quality control and consumer protection were critical dimensions. Certainly, the clinical psychologist was given definite directions for professional functioning. Moreover and where the real challenge was encountered, the clinical psychologist could not allow any source, such as another professional discipline or an administrative policy, to denigrate the standards for the specialty of clinical psychology. As will be discussed subsequently, these same sort of (but different) standards still come from the APA, albeit in varying forms; but now there are other governmental, legal, and commercial (e.g., insurance) sources issuing standards as well.

ETHICAL PRINCIPLES

As discussed in the preceding chapter, ethics emanate from a professional organization and definitely apply only to the members of that organization. Therefore, if a clinical psychologist chose to not be a member of the APA, its ethical principles would not apply to that particular person (i.e., ethics or standards from APA would not necessarily be given legal authority). There are, however, two exceptions to the notion that ethical principles are without legal clout. Let us consider the exceptions in detail.

First, while a set of ethics has no legal authority per se, ethics can be incorporated into a state statute. This may be found in the statutes of certain states that incorporate the APA's (1992a) "Ethical Principles of Psychologists and Code of Conduct" into the law for licensing psychologists. Or, if the ethical principles are not incorporated into the statute by legislative action, the board of examiners can incorporate them, implicitly or explicitly, into their rules via their administrative authority. As one board member said, "No, we do not have the APA ethics as codified standards, but if a complaint against a psychologist has relevance to ethics or standards that board members know have been addressed by APA, there is consideration given to what APA has stated." Also, it is known that certain licensing agencies will actually seek out psychologists knowledgeable of APA ethics and standards to provide information and advisement about prevailing professional practices.

Second, certain civil law cases, such as those that involve an alleged tort (e.g., an injurious wrong done to another person), can hinge upon the standard of care that should have been exercised by the alleged tortfeasor (i.e., an allegedly errant psychologist), and can rely upon ethical principles for defining (at least to some extent) what should or should not have occurred under the circumstances. In other words, ethical principles may be used to help determine whether malpractice occurred. Any action by the psychologist that was not predicated on protecting the welfare of the patient would seemingly be counter to ethical principles, and it is likely that such unethical conduct would carry substantial weight in determining, say, negligence on the part of the therapist.

As these two exceptions illustrate, ethical principles have far-reaching effects. An ethical violation could lead to such detriments as professional censure or loss of one's license to practice, thereby lessening career potential. An ethical violation can also be part of a litigation judgment that imposes a great financial burden, as well as the penalty of having been found guilty of harming a patient.

The "Ethical Principles of Psychologists and Code of Conduct" (APA, 1992a), hereafter referred to as the 1992 ethical principles, are the primary source of ethical and conduct governance for clinical psychologists. There may, however, be other ethical sources to be accommodated. For example, if a clinical psychologist were a member of the American Association for Marriage and Family Therapy (AAMFT) or the American Association of Sex Educators, Counselors, and Therapists (AASECT), his or her practice in the areas of marriage, family, and sex therapy would also fall under the governance of the ethics promulgated by those two organizations. Consequently, if there were a malpractice suit based on alleged faulty provision of marriage, family, or sex therapy, there could be multiple sets of ethics embraced in establishing the standard of care that should have been maintained.

It is noteworthy that the 1992 ethical principles were expanded to being a "Code of Conduct" as well. It seems clear that this expansion was intended to establish standards for practice, including for psychologists outside of APA membership: "The Ethical Standards set forth *enforceable* rules for conduct as psychologists"; and "The Ethics Code is intended to provide standards of professional conduct that can be applied by the APA and by other bodies that choose to adopt them" (p. 1598). In keeping with a code of ethics not being the law, it is acknowledged that: "In the process of making decisions regarding their professional behavior, psychologists must consider this Ethics Code, in addition to applicable laws and psychology board regulations" (p. 1598). While the

1992 ethical principles surely replace previous guidelines, such as the 1981 Specialty Guidelines and the 1987 General Guidelines cited earlier, these historical documents remain useful for assisting present-day interpretations.

The 1992 Ethics Code has a Preamble that is dedicated to the protection and welfare of the individual and society. While "aspirational," the Preamble states that: the goal for psychologists is "to broaden knowledge of behavior and, where appropriate, to apply it pragmatically to improve the condition of both the individual and society"; and the Code "has as its primary goal the welfare and protection of the individuals and groups with whom psychologists work" (p. 1599).

The Code also has "aspirational" General Principles that assert "goals to guide psychologists toward the highest ideals of psychology" (p. 1598). The respective General Principles are revealingly captioned: competence, integrity, professional and scientific responsibility, respect for people's rights and dignity, concern for others' welfare, and social responsibility.

There are eight Ethical Standards, with each containing numerous substandards; they are:

1. General Standards: Applicability of the Ethics Code; Relationship of Ethics and Law; Professional and Scientific Relationship; Boundaries of Competence Maintaining Expertise; Basis for Scientific and Professional Judgments; Describing the Nature and Results of Psychological Services; Human Differences; Respecting Others; Nondiscrimination; Sexual Harassment; Other Harassment; Personal Problems and Conflicts; Avoiding Harm; Misuse of Psychologists' Influence; Misuse of Psychologists' Work; Multiple Relationships; Barter (With Patients or Clients); Exploitative Relationships; Consultations and Referrals; Third-Party Requests for Services; Delegation to and Supervision of Subordinates; Documentation of Professional and Scientific Work; Records and Data; Fees and Financial

Arrangements; Accuracy in Reports to Payors and
Funding Sources; and Referrals and Fees.

2. Evaluation, Assessment, or Intervention: Evaluation,
Diagnosis, and Interventions in Professional Context;
Competence and Appropriate Use of Assessment and
Interventions; Test Construction; Use of Assessment in
General and With Special Populations; Interpreting As-
sessment Results; Unqualified Persons; Obsolete Tests
and Outdated Test Results; Test Scoring and Interpre-
tation Services; Explaining Assessment Results; and
Maintaining Test Security.

3. Advertising and Other Public Statements: Definition
of Public Statements; Statements by Others; Avoidance
of False or Deceptive Statements; Media Presentations;
Testimonials; and In-Person Solicitation.

4. Therapy: Structuring the Relationship; Informed Consent to Therapy; Couple and Family Relationships; Providing Mental Health Services to Those Served by
Others; Sexual Intimacies With Current Patients or
Clients; Therapy With Former Sexual Partners; Sexual
Intimacies With Former Therapy Patients; Interrup-
tion of Services; and Terminating the Professional Relationship.

5. Privacy and Confidentiality: Discussing the Limits of
Confidentiality; Maintaining Confidentiality; Minimiz-
ing Intrusions on Privacy; Maintenance of Records; Dis-
closures; Consultations; Confidential Information in
Databases; Use of Confidential Information for Didac-
tic or Other Purposes; Preserving Records and Data;
Ownership of Records and Data; and Withholding
Records for Nonpayment.

6. Teaching, Training Supervision, Research, and Publishing: Design of Education and Training Programs; Descriptions of Education and Training Programs;
Accuracy and Objectivity in Teaching; Limitation on
Teaching; Assessing Student and Supervisee Performance; Planning Research; Responsibility; Compliance
With Law and Standards; Institutional Approval; Research Responsibilities; Informed Consent to Research;
Dispensing With Informed Consent; Informed Consent
in Research Filming or Recording; Offering Induce-
ments for Research Participants; Deception in Research; Sharing and Utilizing Data; Minimizing
Invasiveness; Providing Participants With Information

About the Study; Honoring Commitments; Care and Use of Animals in Research; Reporting Results; Plagiarism; Publication Credit; Duplicate Publication of Data; Sharing Data; and Professional Reviewers.

7. Forensic Activities: Professionalism; Forensic Assessments; Clarification of Role; Truthfulness and Candor; Prior Relationships; and Compliance With Law and Rules.

8. Resolving Ethical Issues: Familiarity With Ethics Code; Confronting Ethical Issues; Conflicts Between Ethics and Organizational Demands; Informal Resolution of Ethical Violations; Reporting Ethical Violations; Cooperating With Ethical Committees; and Improper Complaints.

While the mere titles for the Ethical Standards and their respective substandards are revealing, it is strongly recommended that every student and practitioner of clinical psychology should read carefully the APA's "Ethical Principles of Psychologists and Code of Conduct," and behave and practice accordingly.

RECENT SPECIALTY GUIDELINES

Since the 1992 APA Ethics Code is quite descriptive and proscriptive, the 1981 Specialty and 1987 General Guidelines discussed earlier have been preempted. In addition, there seems to be a trend for APA, and other regulatory and would-be regulatory sources (e.g., insurance companies), to create guidelines that, while aspirational, essentially become the standards for the particular practice. For example, the APA has adopted "Record Keeping Guidelines" (1993g) and "Guidelines for Child Custody Evaluations in Divorce Proceedings" (1994a); also the APA Ethics Committee has offered a clarifying statement on "Psychotherapy by Telephone" (1993e), which is advanced more formally as being relevant to ethics (American Psychological Association, 1994b). There seems virtually no doubt that there will be more APA guidelines, which will be transformed into standards, forthcoming on a regular basis.

THE FAR-REACHING IMPACT
OF ETHICS

Before further discussion, it is worthwhile to underscore, once again, that an ethics and professional conduct document clearly indicates that the macrolevel is issuing prescriptions and proscriptions for microlevel practice. As explained earlier, micromanagement can become legally codified, thereby applying to psychologists who are not members of the American Psychological Association.

Concern must be expressed about how ethics may foster an intrusion into the clinical psychologist's personal life. Note how certain substandards, such as those under General Standards, can reach to the clinical psychologist's personal values; although it is stated that: "This Ethics Code applies only to psychologists' work-related activities, that is, activities that are part of the psychologists' scientific and professional functions or that are psychological in nature" (p. 1598). That may well be the intent of APA, but it is known that certain other sources, particularly licensing agencies investigating complaints against psychologists, have been known to examine a psychologist's personal conduct (outside of the office, even with persons who have never been clients) according to the view that what goes on personally has impact on professional relationships and services.

Perhaps an intrusion by governmental regulators into the personal life of the licensed clinical psychologist is justified by law and public policy in this era, but suffice it to say that it is certainly different from in the past. This regulatory practice clearly demonstrates how the government, through laws and rules, can potentially intrude into personal rights and liberties. That is, perhaps enjoying the privilege of being a licensed professional carries the concomitant price tag of a lessening of personal freedom in the name of protection (i.e., safety and welfare) of the public, even though the professional's personal rights are presumably protected by the Constitution of the United States.

COMPETENCE

While the total contents of the 1992 Ethics Codes are of critical importance to clinical psychology, special consideration should be given to Principle A: Competence, which states:

> Psychologists strive to maintain high standards of competence in their work. They recognize the boundaries of their particular competencies and the limitations of their expertise. They provide only those services and use only those techniques for which they are qualified by education, training, or experience. Psychologists are cognizant of the fact that the competencies required in serving, teaching, and/or studying groups of people vary with the distinctive characteristics of those groups. In those areas in which recognized professional standards do not yet exist, psychologists exercise careful judgment and take appropriate precautions to protect the welfare of those with whom they work. They maintain knowledge of relevant scientific and professional information related to the services they render, and they recognize the need for ongoing education. Psychologists make appropriate use of scientific, professional, technical, and administrative resources [p. 1599].

This general principle is singled out for emphasis because competence seems interwoven with most, if not all, ethical standards, as well as the mores, values, ethics, and laws critical to the practice of clinical psychology. If the clinical psychologist studiously adhered to the nuances of competence, professional performance would be virtually flawless.

ETHICAL COMPLAINTS

If there is an alleged ethical violation, tradition has it that the complaining psychologist should talk to the colleague who is believed to have been in violation of the ethical code. For example, Standard 8.04—Informal Resolution of Ethical Violations states: "When psychologists believe that there may have been an ethical violation by another psychologist, they attempt to resolve the issue by bringing it to the attention of the individual if an informal resolution appears appropriate and the intervention does not violate any confidentiality rights that may be involved" (p. 1611). This is a traditional approach, which may or may not prove to be viable today. In this litigious era, such confrontations carry a risk. For example, the psychologist whose performance is being questioned may be indignant toward or even threaten legal action against the complaining psychologist.

In any event, it now seems best to carry all complaints, whether between two professionals or between a layperson and a professional, to a professional ethics committee or to a state licensing board. Standard 8.05—Reporting Ethical Violations states: "If an apparent ethical violation is not appropriate for informal resolution under Standard 8.04 or is not resolved properly in that fashion, psychologists take further action appropriate to the situation, unless such action conflicts with confidentiality rights in ways that cannot be resolved. Such action may include referral to state or national committees on professional ethics or to state licensing boards" (p. 1611).

In other words, notwithstanding the negatives that it may create for the reporting psychologist, the APA member (and possibly nonmembers, depending on the state licensing law and rules) has an ethical responsibility to report another psychologist believed to be in violation of ethics. Moreover, Standard 8.06—Cooperating with Ethics Committees sets forth that: "Psychologists cooperate in ethics investigations, proceedings, and resulting requirements of the APA or any affiliated state psychological association to which they belong. In doing so, they make reasonable efforts to resolve any issues as to confidentiality. Failure to cooperate is itself an ethics violation" (p. 1611).

Clearly, there is a profound policing responsibility being imposed upon the psychologist. There is also a modern legal trend toward creating a mandatory duty for a licensed psychologist to report possible statutory or rule violations by another licensed psychologist to the appropriate state agency, such as the licensing board (note that, to date, this duty does not exist in every state).

It is known that some psychologists have initiated, encouraged, or filed ethics complaints for less than honorable reasons. Often it seems that the reporting psychologist assumes a somewhat pretentious piety for "protecting society," when in actuality the underlying motive is an attempt to discredit another psychologist who has been a competitor in the mental health marketplace.

The law seldom allows a ready remedy for a respondent who has been subjected to a false or inadequately based complaint. In an extreme case (involving blatantly false and malicious conduct by the reporting psychologist), a counter legal action might be possible. It is hoped that professional integrity will preclude or deter wrongful reporting of complaints. In general, the only practical protection that the respondent receives is the proscription contained in Standard 8.07—Improper Complaints, namely: "Psychologists do not file or encourage the filing of ethical complaints that are frivolous and are intended to harm the respondent rather than protect the public" (p. 1611).

RULES AND PROCEDURES
FOR ETHICAL COMPLAINTS

Today, there seems to be a trend away from ethical complaints and toward complaints to regulatory agencies, such as the licensing board. Even in the realm of ethical complaints, there is a trend away from conducting the proceedings at the local level (a number of state psychological associations no longer attempt adjudication of ethics complaints) and toward proceedings at the national level. Nonetheless, there is still the possibility of ethical actions at the local or state level, at least in some geographical areas.

The exact route for an ethics complaint depends, to some degree, on the nature of the complaint and the geographical location of the psychologist. There are other types of ethical violations that could potentially be cleared up, to the advantage of all concerned, by informal communications. Certain locales have local or regional ethics committees from which a decision could possibly be appealed to a state-level ethics committee, which in turn could possibly be appealed to a national-level ethics committee—and there are many other feasible committee routes. Moreover, there are some ethical violations which might best be handled by bypassing ethics committees altogether, and be transformed into a criminal and/or civil lawsuit. For complaints involving APA members, the rules and procedures are provided in APA publications (APA, 1992b, 1996). The APA Ethics Committee (1994b) regularly publishes a report that describes, among other things, revisions, the types of complaints received and processed, and the outcomes of the adjudications.

Before leaving the matter of ethics and guidelines, it should be noted that the national health care reform movement supports professional guidelines. For example, the Agency for Health Care Policy and Research believes that, given significant practice variations, there should be "the development of science-based clinical guidelines, performance measures, and standards of quality" (Clinton, McCormick, and Besteman, 1994, p. 30). Accordingly, the Agency recently published practice guidelines on depression in primary care settings (Munoz, Hollon, McGrath, Rehm, and VandenBos, 1994). Given the health care reform propositions that practitioners must adhere to clear-cut standards and regulatory sources must monitor the performance of services (Starr, 1994), it seems assured that guidelines and standards will proliferate.

PROFESSIONAL STANDARDS REVIEW COMMITTEES

Some state associations sponsor a professional standards review committee (PSRC). Such a committee receives complaints about a psychologist's practice, and provides mediation or arbitration to resolve the matter; informal or formal hearings may be held. Any opinion issued is commonly considered advisory, such as stating what might be deemed "usual and customary" for the practice that is in question (Claiborn, 1982). In the array of regulatory sources, the Professional Standards Review Committee does not occupy a prominent spot. From a professional viewpoint, recapturing self-regulation for the professional discipline would seemingly be promoted by use of the Professional Standards Review Committee option; however, the general demise of any sort of immunity, even for something as honorable as a professional review of standards, leaves liability that few psychologists would willingly accept.

While there is certain logic to having a peer review committee, health care reform does not show deference; the negativism toward self-determination by health care providers (Starr, 1994) likely spawns a "no honor among thieves" viewpoint by governmental sources. For example, Gardner and Wilcox (1993) point out how political intervention occurs in scientific peer review. The health care reform movement supports further political influence on and determination of the procedures for establishing standards.

THIRD-PARTY PAYER
QUALITY ASSURANCE

Major health plans, such as those available through the federal government or through insurance companies, can potentially include third-party reimbursement to the patient-policyholder for the services provided by clinical psychologists. Ostensibly, in order to maintain control of the quality of services that will be reimbursed (and perhaps to lessen the number of practitioners who will qualify for third-party payments), health plans have implemented rules.

An insurance policy could exclude mental health services, unless the policyholder paid a premium for such special coverage. Or an insurance policy could restrict payment for only those mental health services provided by psychiatrists and psychologists (thereby excluding, say, clinical social workers). Note that many states have "freedom of choice" legislation that specifies, for example, that if a medical physician is eligible for reimbursement, so shall a licensed psychologist be eligible for reimbursement. In other words, the policyholder has a right to seek treatment from any relevant health care provider licensed by the state. Or an insurance policy may provide payment only for those psychologists who have been designated "clinical" psychologists, such as by special certification through the state board of psychology examiners (note that such a distinction by state licensing is on the wane) or by the American Board of Professional Psychology (ABPP) or by the National Register of Health Care Providers in Psychology. Eligibility by special "clinical" qualifications seems to be less relied upon by insurance companies, with deference being given to state licensure. Of course, state licensure has, in turn, tended toward more emphasis on clinical qualifications, regardless of the doctoral specialty of the licensing applicant.

Even after the services of a clinical psychologist have been deemed eligible for coverage, the insurance carrier may maintain a review of the treatment program. By careful review of the treatment program, fraud can be avoided, and the treatment approach can be monitored for appropriateness and quality. These evaluative judgments are generally made by clinical psychologists or other mental health professionals employed as reviewers. It is known, however, that some utilization reviews occur without a professional from the same discipline as the service provider. For example, the review of clinical psychology may be conducted by a clerk or nurse, with an orientation to mental health standards and supervised by a physician (not necessarily a psychiatrist). It is interesting to note that: "Even when utilization review leads to the conclusion that incompetent treatment has occurred, the usual disposition is to deny reimbursement for the individual case alone and to take no further action against the incompetent provider" (Claiborn, 1982, p. 154).

The utilization review relies heavily on documentation, namely the clinical records. Consequently, some insurance carriers are promulgating records guidelines, which must be satisfied to be eligible for reimbursement (Woody, 1994b). Unfortunately, it is known that clinical psychologists manifest inconsistency in the quality of their record-keeping practices (Fulero and Wilbert, 1988), which likely contributed to the APA's (1993g) publishing guidelines on record keeping.

Returning to the issue of insurance companies as regulatory sources, some wags have asserted that third-party reimbursement will create too much use of mental health service. Contrary to other findings, DeMuth and Kamis (1980) obtained data that contradicted the belief that third-party insurance payments encouraged overutilization. They found use was not dependent on economic or provider variables: "Availability of public third-party reimbursement did not lead to excessive service utilization by needy, severely disturbed clients" (p. 795). The amount of the fee, the patient's sociodemographic profile, and the provider's characteristics offered little explanation for the service utilization patterns that were found.

At the risk of sounding crass, there is no doubt that third-party payments have enhanced the financial aspects of clinical psychology practice. At the same time, it is believed that it has had a constructive regulatory impact on the profession, for the benefit of the client-patient and of society.

With the elimination of a stigma regarding psychotherapy, the provision of mental health services constitutes a sizable industry. Magaro, Gripp, and McDowell (1978) offer a historicoeconomic analysis of the mental health industry. They conclude that the best system is one in which there would be "the cessation of automatic funding of all publicly maintained mental institutions" (p. 220). Instead, they endorse "a return of competitive capitalism in the mental health industry" (p. 218). This free enterprise economic arena would mean that "the funds would be reserved for disbursal to treaters according to the degree of rehabilitation, improvement, or 'success' they facilitate in their clients" (p. 220). The stance taken by Magaro, Gripp, and McDowell supports the view that the quality assurance efforts of the third-party payer should have a positive effect for all concerned.

In the 1990s, the foremost third-party payment sources are managed health care programs (e.g., health maintenance organizations [HMOs], preferred provider organizations [PPOs], and Employee Assistance Programs [EAPs]). Of course health insurance underlies managed health care, so the two entities are intertwined.

No matter what nice language is used, it is incontrovertible that managed health care programs are devoted to cost reduction for the payment sources, namely the insurance companies or other underwriting funds. While managed health care presumably provides protection to consumers by monitoring the quality of health care services provided, each program typically has strict limits on the services that can be provided under its financial coverage and no accommodation of quality care per se: "Managed care legislation to date has established few parameters for ensuring the delivery of quality mental health services" (Newman and Bricklin, 1991). Quite regularly, the clinical psychologist will encounter a client who needs more or different treatment than is allowed by the managed health care program. Not being able to continue treatment is obviously detrimental to the client, and creates liability for the clinical psychologist (Applebaum, 1993).

Many clinical psychologists, and other health care providers as well, believe that true concern for the quality of service or the well-being of the consumer or patient is minimal, with the emphasis on cost containment and reduction. Woody (1991) states: "Notwithstanding a cost containment objective from third-party payment sources, the mental health practitioner should maintain that quality care does not allow nonprofessional reasoning, such as a subservience to cost containment, at the expense of training-based logic, reasoning, and judgment" (p. 16). Unfortunately, the clinical psychologist's attempt to influence the managed health care program is most often a David versus Goliath scenario, with an absence of slings and pebbles.

When considering the cost reduction versus quality assurance issue, the specter of more regulatory guidelines arises. Somewhat illogically, the onus is primarily on the practitioner as opposed to the dictator of practices, to wit the managed health care program. Newman and Bricklin (1991) say: "It is difficult, if not impossible, to screen out those providers who will sacrifice quality for financial rewards, but appropriate ethical parameters for provider behavior can minimize such abuses" (p. 31). To date, the profession of psychology has not offered a set of "ethical parameters" that will afford the practitioner authority in the face of denial of eligibility by the managed health care program.

Being financial institutions, managed health care sources are not apologetic. Haas and Cummings (1991) are aligned with a promanaged health care position, and urge clinical psychologists to consider carefully whether to affiliate with a managed health care program. It is common for any objection about managed health care operations from a clinical psychologist to be countered by a denial of eligibility. The financial dilemma is, of course, that there has been a rapid escalation of control of the health care marketplace by managed health care programs (in some states more than others), and pragmatics may dictate that the clinical psychologist (especially if primarily reliant upon private practice) must affiliate with managed health care programs in order to have an adequate financial underpinning.

STATE LICENSING BOARDS AND REGULATORY AGENCIES

Through legislation, a state controls employment in its jurisdiction via the granting of licenses and permits. Sometimes there is similar regulation by other governmental entities, such as at the county or municipality level. This regulatory function is intended to assure quality and safeguard the citizenry, but it may also generate financial revenue for the governmental entity.

A state board of examiners of psychologists administers the licensing program. This board is typically comprised of psychologists and laypersons (the latter are intended to keep the profession aware of the public voice), with legal counsel always present. The board may be under the administrative aegis of a larger state department, namely a department responsible for professional regulation. For example, the regulation of psychology in the State of Florida rests with the Department of Business and Professional Regulation (DBPR), which is under the Agency for Health Care Administration (AHCA). Such an umbrella department generally oversees a number of disciplinary boards.

The authority of the board is created by statutory law. Certain qualifications for licensure and practice are specified, usually in terms of academic training and supervised experience. The area of practice is defined, and the procedures for examination are set forth. Misconduct, violations, penalties, exemptions, and renewal matters may be delineated.

An interesting dovetailing of regulatory efforts can be found when a state licensing board restricts those psychologists deemed eligible to sit for the examination to those who have graduated from APA-accredited training programs (or the equivalent). To the consternation of some higher education authorities, this APA-statutory combination could effectively regulate the university's standards for training psychologists.

Another important trend is continuing education. More and more states are predicating the renewal of a license upon the psychologist's having completed a certain number of continuing education hours.

Nowadays, staying current is both an ethical and legal matter. Unless there is documentation of continuing education, the assumption (in some states) is that the psychologist's knowledge of current scientific and professional information has become outdated to the point where the public welfare would best be served by denying the renewal of his or her license to practice.

At this point in time, there seems no doubt that the foremost regulatory source for the licensed psychologist is the state agency that is legislatively assigned the duty to police the profession. It should be recognized that state licensing is not intended to enhance the status or income of the practitioner, it is to provide governmental monitoring and regulation of the licensed profession. By law, the regulatory agency can award and take away the right to practice in the particular state. States vary in the emphasis placed on the regulation of psychology. The trend is, however, definitely toward greater regulation and more severe penalties for violations of the prevailing standards. For example, Woody (1994a) analyzes the regulatory complaints against psychologists in Florida and reports: "the foregoing percentages suggest that over, say, the next five years, about one-third of Licensed Psychologists will be the subject of a DBPR formal complaint" (p. 19).

Many psychologists incorrectly believe that, if there is a complaint, the licensing board is a group of colleagues who will show deference to the psychologist. Without exception, the state licensing board focuses on accountability to safeguard the consumer—there is no peer deference. As Stampelos and Jones (1990) tell attorneys, "No matter how pleasant the department's representatives may be, they are not there to do your client a favor" (p. 68). When faced with a complaint to the licensing board, the wise clinical psychologist recognizes that it is an adversarial disciplinary proceeding that necessitates a vigorous legal defense, making use of an attorney to maximize the possibility of coping successfully with the maze of legal formalities that are beyond the training of the clinical psychologist (Benton, 1988; Wyckoff, 1990). If probable cause for discipline is found by the state regulatory agency, the penalty on the clinical psychologist can be profound and lifelong. In addition to any diminution of professional status (e.g., a drop in reputation), income (e.g., suspension or revocation of license), and expense (e.g., a fine, the cost of supervision), there will be the requirement of potentially reporting the violation to other licensing boards, professional associations, quality control committees (e.g., with third-party payment and employment sources), and malpractice insurance carriers.

NATIONAL REGISTER

Another form of regulation of clinical psychologists emanates from the *National Register of Health Service*

Providers in Psychology (Council for the National Register of Health Service Providers in Psychology, 1993), hereafter referred to as the National Register. The National Register appears in the form of a directory: "over 16,000 psychologists who voluntarily applied, were approved for listing and completed the process as of August 31, 1993" (p. I-1). Applicants submit their credentials for evaluation according to criteria intended to assure competency in providing health services.

To be approved for the National Register, the applicant must:

> (1) be currently licensed, certified, or registered by a State/ Provincial Board of Examiners of Psychology at the independent practice level of psychology; (2) have completed a doctoral degree in psychology from a regionally accredited educational institution; and (3) have completed two years (3,000 hours) of supervised experience in health services in psychology, of which one year (1,500 hours) is in an organized health service training program or internship and one year (1,500 hours) is at the postdoctoral level [p. I-2].

The Council offers the following definition: "A Health Service Provider in Psychology is defined as a psychologist, licensed/certified/registered at the independent practice level in his/her jurisdiction, who is trained and experienced in the delivery of direct, preventive, assessment and therapeutic intervention services to individuals whose growth, adjustment, or functioning is impaired or to individuals who otherwise seek services" (p. I-3).

The National Register has come to be recognized as a source for sorting out the qualified independent clinical practitioners from the self-proclaimed clinical practitioners. That is, the National Register evaluates an applicant's credentials to assure consonance with the established standards for health care providers in psychology.

Other professional sources turn to the National Register for guidance. For example, an insurance company might look to the National Register when deciding whether a clinical psychologist is eligible for third-party reimbursement. Or a clinical psychologist who has a client moving to another state might consult the National Register to locate the name of a clinical psychologist in the new locale to whom the client can be referred for continued treatment. In keeping with the regulatory function, the National Register provides for "deleting from listing any Registrant who had been found to violate the guidelines approved by the National Register Board of directors related to professional conduct" (p. I-18). Among other things, this includes "professional misconduct, conviction of a serious crime, malpractice, and becoming professionally incapacitated or disabled" (p. I-18). Note how a disciplinary action by, say, a state regulatory agency would extend the negative consequences to remaining on the National Registry.

DIPLOMATE STATUS

Since diplomate status was discussed in detail in the preceding chapter, the subject will only be summarized here. As will be recalled, becoming "diplomated" refers to a clinical psychologist's having passed a peer review for expertise in a specialty. This review might be based only on an analysis of the "paper credentials" of the candidate, or— as would be the case with the more prestigious diplomating boards—it would include an analysis of the credentials and a work sample, as a prerequisite for a written or oral examination.

At the present time, there are numerous specialties that have a relevant diplomating program. As detailed in the preceding chapter, the most honorific source is the American Board of Professional Psychology (ABPP), which has an examination process for becoming a diplomate in the specialties of clinical psychology, counseling psychology, school psychology, clinical neuropsychology, family psychology, behavioral psychology, health psychology, forensic psychology, industrial-organizational psychology, and group psychology. There is the possibility that other specialties will be added in the future.

The status of diplomate creates a press for competency: "The American Board of Professional Psychology (ABPP) diploma is seen by some as a means to encourage a higher level of ability by defining a higher 'floor' of competence, which may prove helpful to the public in assessing competence" (Claiborn, 1982, p. 155).

Much like a listing in the National Register, the ABPP diplomate status might be expected for third-party reimbursement from an insurance company (although some states have statutes that could limit the type of qualifying restrictions that an insurance company could maintain), or might lead a clinical psychologist to give referral preference to a practitioner in another part of the country to which one of his or her clients is moving. Moreover, some states recognize the ABPP diplomate in the licensing–certification requirements. For example, an examination might be waived if the applicant were an ABPP diplomate.

While the foregoing regulatory sources might seem like a plethora of safeguards, there are weaknesses in the system. As Claiborn (1982) summarizes:

> There are no centralized, standardized, organized means to define or detect incompetence; no accepted mechanisms to define it; few mechanisms for adjudication in cases of suspected incompetence; and few sanctions available for cases of proven incompetence. None of the contextual definitions of incompetence . . . include consideration of the following as bases for determining professional competencies: treatment outcomes; relative efficiency of treatments; safety and efficacy of treatments; or treatment plan, that is, did the plan have a reasonable, conceptual, and empirical linking of goal, method, and outcome [p. 155].

There is, however, a final source of regulation of clinical psychology that intervenes when peer-review regulation fails, namely, the legal system.

LEGAL JUDGMENT OF CLINICAL PSYCHOLOGY

The American legal system is devoted to maintaining social order: "It is a dynamic process by which rules are constantly being adopted and changed to fit the complex situations of a developing society" (Grilliot, 1975, p. 3). As reflected throughout this book, clinical psychology has moved rapidly and is very much a part of contemporary society's development and complexity. Consequently, society has expanded its legal umbrella over the practice of clinical psychology:

> As society recognizes a profession, it imposes upon that discipline a concomitant responsibility or duty—a set of expectations as to what should and should not occur in professional practice. In other words, the *quid pro quo* for societal recognition of professionalism is professional accountability to society. When society judges professional practice to be substandard, it attaches legal liability. It is this interface between public policy and professionalism which creates the legal framework for malpractice [Woody, 1985, pp. 509–510].

In other words, society has an expectation of high quality care from those to whom it gives a virtual monopoly for a service via its professional licensing. When the professional breaches the standard, society asks its legal arm to reach out and impose sanctions, such as by withdrawing professional status (e.g., eliminating the license) or seeking compensation for the injured person (e.g., imposing a court-ordered judgment for damages emanating from the malpractice). "Being a care-giving professional, the concomitant accountability opens the courtroom door to any person who believes that he or she has suffered damage as a result of the practitioner" (Woody, LaVoie, and Epps, 1992, p. 353).

Clinical psychology can have the bitter-sweet satisfaction of knowing that its professionalism is well established, as documented by the number of lawsuits that are filed against its practitioners. According to Fisher (1985), from 1955 to 1965 (the first 10 years that the APA offered malpractice coverage), no claims were filed against psychologists; from 1976 to 1981, there were 266 claims (an average of 44 per year); from 1982 to 1984, the annual rate more than tripled (an average of 153 claims per year); "the number of claims against psychologists have risen faster in the past three years than for any other mental health profession" (p. 6); and "In the past two years, the number of sexual malpractice suits against psychologists have multiplied by five, so that they represent 20 to 30 percent of all suits, and cost insurers twice as much as all other causes combined" (p. 7).

Psychologists are sued for many reasons. Hogan (1979) analyzed legal allegations against psychotherapists (not just clinical psychologists), and found:

> In the 300 cases collected here, more than twenty-five types of actions were brought, including involuntary serviture, false arrest, trespass, malicious infliction of emotional distress, abuse of process, loss of liberty, misrepresentation, libel, assault and battery, malicious prosecution, and false imprisonment. Outnumbering all actions put together, however, is the simple negligence or malpractice suit, which occurs in more than two-thirds of the cases [p. 7].

Stated differently, this analysis reveals that: (1) psychotherapists are not exempt from sociobehavioral frailty; and (2) the legal system imposes a standard of care for professional practice.

Malpractice is predicated on failure to maintain a standard of care; stated more specifically:

> *Malpractice is the failure to fulfill the requisite standard of care.* Malpractice can occur by *omission* (what should have been done, but was not done) or *commission* (doing something that should not have been done). In either case, the act is not subject to a malpractice legal action unless

it satisfies the elements of negligence, namely that there was a duty which was breached and which caused injury to a person to whom the duty was owed, and damages can be used to remedy the tortious infringement on the injured person's rights [Woody, 1988a, pp. 2–3].

In succinct terms: "The quality of professional care is required legally to meet the standard of minimum knowledge, skill, and intelligence common to members of the profession" (Woody, 1983b, p. 1435); and "As for professional standards of conduct, the practitioner need not be superior but must possess and exercise the knowledge and skill of a member of the profession in good standing" (Woody, 1984, p. 393).

For the conscientious clinical psychologist, there are safeguards for avoiding malpractice (Woody, 1983a, 1988a,b, 1991). On the other hand, the litigious era is such that even the conscientious practitioner is not immune from a lawsuit. Indeed, there is reason to believe that many lawsuits are filed by patients who are dissatisfied for dubious reasons, such as suddenly deciding that the clinical psychologist did not exercise an adequate standard of care only when an attempt is made to make the patient pay an overdue treatment bill (Wright, 1981a,b).

Given the risk of litigation, today's clinical psychologist should not take a complaint from a dissatisfied client casually. Rather, any complaint should be countered with a defensive strategy:

The prudent human services professional should (1) have a clear delineation of the standard of care that would be applied to his or her services; (2) adopt assessment procedures to ensure that the services were reasonably tailored to the needs of the client and were consonant with the standard of care; (3) maintain a system by which clients are informed about and consent to the professional interventions; and (4) consistently exercise safeguards against any knowing or inadvertent deviations from or any real or imagined breaches of the established standard of care [Woody, 1984, p. 400].

Numerous guidelines for quality care are provided in Woody (1988b, 1991).

It should be readily evident that, if peer-review regulatory functions fail, the legal system affords society a final means for regulating professional practices. Given the mushrooming number of lawsuits against professionals of every ilk, it would appear that the legal system is keenly sensitive to societal concerns about regulation, as would be applied to clinical psychology (along with many other professional disciplines). From the standpoint of social theory: "It is unprofessional to attempt to deny, consciously or unconsciously, that these public policy legal sanctions are justified" (Woody, 1984, p. 401).

Aside from malpractice, the legal system can also regulate the specific practices within a profession. As a cogent example, clinical psychologists predicate many of their interventions, particularly psychotherapy, on maintaining confidentiality. Going further, state statutes typically extend confidentiality into privileged communication between clinical psychologist and his or her client. That is, public policy endorses, through its laws, that the relationship between the clinical psychologist and a patient is so sacrosanct that others cannot have access to its contents.

Even though a privileged communication statute might deem the clinical psychologist–patient relationship sacrosanct, the legal system may sanction exceptions. For example, the court's subpoena power can be used to obtain a clinical psychologist's records or testimony about a patient embroiled in a legal controversy. In other words, public policy supports that sometimes the right to social justice supersedes the right to confidentiality or privileged communication.

Recall the comments by the psychologist in the opening section of this chapter, where the psychologist was reluctant to be involved in legal proceedings because "I know the father just intends to use what I say against the mother in court." This is an example of how the interests of social justice supersede the right to confidentiality or privileged communication.

While the focus of this section is on the regulation of clinical psychology, it should be noted that clients are often unable to differentiate between privacy as an ethical versus a legal concept (McGuire, Toal, and Blau, 1985). The complexity of the law and the characteristics of clients combine to construct a difficult problem: "The challenge to practitioners . . . is how to provide accurate, impartial, and comprehensive information to clients who vary so widely in their ability to understand" (Muehleman, Pickens, and Robinson, 1985, p. 396). The inconsistencies, contradictions, and exceptions within the law governing privileged communication led Knapp and VandeCreek (1985) to assert: "Until these laws are changed, psychologists will practice under the current patchwork of existing laws" (p. 405). Needless to say, anything that is "patchwork" does not give a solid composition. There are many ambiguities inherent to the clinical psychologist's allegiance to confidentiality and privileged communication.

CASE ANALYSIS

At the beginning of this chapter, a brief case was presented, for which the message is clear-cut: a clinical psychologist can neither be self-determining nor practice solely by professional ethics. Even with the best interests of the client in mind, the clinical psychologist must submit to the regulatory power of many sources, particularly as required by law. Standards for providers, ethical codes, professional standards review committees, third-party payer quality assurance efforts, state licensing and certification boards, the National Register, diplomate status, and, perhaps foremost, the legal system exert unyielding pressure on virtually every element of the practice of clinical psychology. The pressure never ceases, as exemplified by the renewal of a license to practice being predicated (in more and more states) on the psychologist's fulfilling a continuing education requirement. Lest this seem inappropriate, it must be remembered that professionalism is a product of society, and regulatory sources are society's servants for maintaining public welfare.

Chapter 8

The Future of Preparation and Employment in Clinical Psychology

Looking to the future, there is no clear picture of training and employment in clinical psychology. As indicated throughout this book, clinical psychology has been evolving constantly, and if anything, there is reason to believe that the change will be even more profound in the foreseeable future.

Today's somewhat tumultuous health care conditions do not constitute a harbinger of doom for health care in general or clinical psychology in specific. To the contrary, the current health care scenario can best be appreciated as an unprecedented opportunity to advance health care services, and as well discussed, clinical psychology is poised to enjoy the greatest of possible outcomes. As Charles Dickens said, "these are the best of times, these are the worst of times." This chapter will examine what may seem like the worst of conditions, namely, those emanating from health care reform and managed health care systems, and provide information about how to transform them into the best of conditions for clinical psychologists.

SELF-DEFEATING BEHAVIOR

Winston Churchill is credited with having said, "We have met the enemy, and it is ourselves." Despite the science, knowledge, and insight upon which psychology is based, there have been, regrettably, certain tendencies to act in a manner that contradicts success and progress for the discipline.

One of the major problems has arisen from claims of benefits from psychological strategies that cannot be documented empirically. Jacobson (1995) states: "False prophets are easy to recognize. They expect you to trust their clinical judgment, while showing no signs of humility or doubts about the wisdom of what they are proselytizing." Too often, psychology has allowed false prophets. Of course, it can be and has been worse, as exemplified by the innumerable incidents involving scientists' "cooking" (falsifying) data. In a private conversation, one nationally known family therapist responded to a question about a particular therapeutic technique that he espoused by saying, "There's a lot of stuff in my books that I never actually use in therapy—if I did I would probably get sued for malpractice—but I published the ideas to sell books."

Questionable conduct, spurred on by the true meaning of behavioral science, has paved the way for more formal evaluations and criticisms. Certainly research on the efficacy of psychotherapy has fostered doubts. The basic question is whether or not treatment effects are superior to placebo effects or no treatment, and research has yet to provide a definitive answer. Wierzbicki (1993) provides a reasonably balanced review of these studies, and concludes that "The quality of the controlled research has improved" (p. 44). Dawes (1994) broadens the scope of inquiry to considering, in addition to the effects of psychotherapy, the presumed expertise of mental health professionals when it comes to making predictions and diagnoses, relying on experience, using licensing as a tool for protecting the public, and so on. The dubious benefits from various mental health practices highlights what may well be a major future role for clinical psychologists, to wit conducting accountability research. More will be said on this issue later.

FUTURE MENTAL HEALTH SERVICE SYSTEMS

The inauguration of the Clinton administration was the advent of heightened public policy concern about health care. The fundamental purpose was, ostensibly, to assure that all people would receive quality care. It soon emerged, however, that the primary agenda was cost containment (or preferably reduction), and the assurance of quality care appeared secondary at best. From the vantage point of the Clinton administration, Starr (1994) made it clear that health care practitioners were not to be trusted, pointing out how their costs had soared, and how alternative (read lesser trained) practitioners could be used.

For political reasons, government-centered health care reform at the national level was set aside in 1994. Regardless, health care reform continues, albeit more within third-party payment sources and state governments than at the national governmental level. As McFall (1995) puts it: "The Clinton administration's failed proposals notwithstanding, reform of our nation's health care system not only is inevitable, it already is underway. The question is no longer *whether* but *how* it will be accomplished" (p. B-1). There seems little or no doubt that health care reform, especially under the aegis of commercialized managed health care systems, will be critical to the future of clinical psychology.

In approaching the issues of health care reform and commercialized managed health care systems in the future, the criticisms of clinical psychology, such as about the efficacy of psychotherapy, should be recalled. The criticisms may well be blessings in disguise for clinical psychologists.

McFall (1995) says: "The first step in reform should be to identify psychology's legitimate and unique roles in a well-designed health-care system. Two related questions must be asked: First, which of psychology's purported contributions have been shown by empirical research to be valid? Second, which services can psychologists perform significantly better than other mental-health professionals or paraprofessionals?" (p. B-2). Since clinical psychologists are peerless in their ability to apply behavioral science to their services, it seems logical that they can move to the forefront in establishing accountability, be it for their discipline or for other health care disciplines.

It appears that clinical psychologists can become, in a sense, the "super clinician," providing essential management along with clinical services. Cummings (1995) believes that: "the future doctoral-level psychologist is in an excellent position to conduct outcome research and to plan and implement effective and efficient delivery systems in an expanded clinical management role" (p. 15). Relevant to training, this means that graduate programs will need to give emphasis to preparing clinical scientists capable of conducting research that defines and advances assessment and treatment for all mental health practitioners, and most certainly themselves. Relevant to employment, this means that graduate programs will need to make changes: "Psychology programs and faculties must face the realities of future manpower needs as well. Because we will need fewer Ph.D. psychologists to provide direct services, the total number of students and faculty members involved in doctoral training should decrease. Yet we simultaneously will need to expand the supply of clinical researchers evaluating the efficacy of various treatments" (McFall, 1995, p. B-3). With all due respect to McFall's opinion about the dwindling number of providers of direct service, which may or may not be true, the possibility of increasing the roles and services of clinical psychology could actually accommodate an increase in both direct service providers and clinical researchers. Returning to the notion of blessings in disguise, the criticisms of mental health services coupled with health care reform, however viewed, seem to enhance future training and employment opportunities in clinical psychology.

Psychology as a "cottage industry" is no more. At this time, there are 556 HMOs nationwide, with continual mergers and other changes in data. Belar (1995) states: "Physician hospital organizations (PHOs) will most likely dominate the piecemeal delivery systems common today, as only such integrated systems are capable of providing the comprehensive, seamless care consumers are demanding" (p. 139); and under a capitated model, "rather than providing only what one knows how to do, the practitioner is challenged to think about what he or she needs to learn how to do, how to most efficiently manage professional time and treatment resources, how services should be delivered, and what kinds of colleagues should be available to provide needed services" (p. 140). The latter supports that training will have to be lifelong, which will require faculty members to focus more on continuing professional education and students/practitioners being dedicated to acquiring new knowledge and skills throughout their careers.

The individual practitioner and the employing organization alike must be mindful of quality assurance and of earning acceptance by governmental and managed health care sources. Coalitions are being formed to consolidate purchasing power, with "report cards" being issued to reveal a particular practitioner's efficacy and type of services. Employers of workers receiving coverage for their mental health needs are demanding accountability. As a result, the HMO-Employer Data Information System (HEDIS) has been formed; it requires managed health care organizations to report indicators of care and usage, member satisfaction with care, and financial performance.

The future will introduce more specifications about what psychological services will be covered by third-party payment sources. From the vantage point of the insurance industry, Broskowski (1995) states: "We can no longer dismiss some standardization of what we practice by glibly calling it 'cookbook' psychology. When food is scarce and people are starving, society would greatly prefer a cookbook with simple recipes for combating malnutrition to employing the services of some creative chefs demanding an unlimited budget for the best gourmet food suited to their highly developed palates" (pp. 160–161). He also says: "More emphasis should be placed on models of mental health and illness that view anxiety, depression, and many forms of maladaptive behaviors as episodic conditions requiring brief intervention and subsequent repeat interventions on an as-needed basis, much like primary care providers currently view the common cold and minor physical ailments" (p. 161). It can be expected that this orientation will create discomfort for some trainers and practitioners, but like it or not, it must be accommodated.

Future health care will be under increasingly governmental regulation (recall the discussion of regulatory agencies and licensing boards in the preceding chapter). Governmental regulation and commercialized managed health care systems increase the legal liability for the clinical psychologist (Appelbaum, 1993). This means that, along with likely decreases in payments for services per se, the clinical psychologist will encounter increased costs for legal and accounting consultants (e.g., to fulfill required governmental reporting, to understand or negotiate a contract with a managed health care company) and insurance (e.g., to cover the indemnification that is commonly assigned to the practitioner by a managed health care contract). Stated differently, the practice of clinical psychology in the future will necessitate new legal and business knowledge on the part of the practitioner, as well as additional expenses for operating a practice or agency.

There is reason to doubt that trainers have, to date, accepted this legal–business filter through which clinical psychology passes in the modern day. Informal surveys reveal that the large majority of clinical psychologists believe that they lack adequate preparation in legal and business issues.

Governmental regulation will introduce more prescriptions and proscriptions for the provision of clinical psychology services. There is already the Agency For Health Care Policy and Research (AHCPR), which is a Federal agency under the U.S. Department of Health and Human Services, that promulgates clinical practice guidelines. While little has been done in mental health to date (see Munoz, Hollon, McGrath, Rehm, and VandenBos, 1994; Schulberg and Rush, 1994), clinical practice guidelines relevant to psychological services are emerging. Relatedly and as discussed in the preceding chapter, professional associations are adopting practice guidelines that will surely increase in number and specificity. All of these efforts will result in the clinical psychologist having less self-determination about how to provide services to clients and to shoulder increased legal liability.

With the lack of self-determination on the part of the clinical psychologist, there is reason to question whether a client's idiosyncratic needs will be subverted by managed health care policy limits. For example, it is common for a managed health care program to restrict the number of outpatient psychotherapy sessions. Karon (1995b) believes that the clients will eventually oppose and require adjustments of these restrictions: "Patients learned before, as they will again now, that six sessions for everything is not psychotherapy; that therapists who are willing to pretend that six sessions for everything is reasonable do not even do those six sessions well; and if they want help, they must escape managed care" (p. 8). Given the power of financial control possessed by the managed health care company, Karon's view may be unrealistic for the short run, but in the future this interface of client need versus corporate determinations will surely be subject to restructuring.

THE POSITIVE FUTURE

Managed health care systems do not necessarily have to impact negatively on employment of clinical psychologists, but significant adaptation in training and personal goals will be necessary. Hersch (1995) believes that "there is reason to believe that the long-term prognosis for psychological practice is excellent" (p. 24), and recommends three directions that should be pursued:

> The first direction is to explore the possibilities for diversifying practice, both within the health care environment and in other contexts, such as business. . . . The second major direction for change is in the organization and administration of psychological practices into larger, more integrated, and more comprehensive units. . . . The third direction requires psychologists to be more active in the process of outcome evaluation in order to direct clinical practice and document the efficacy of practice [p. 25].

These three directions certainly seem appropriate and essential to successful employment in the future.

Within the realm of professionalism, the clinical psychologist should not believe that there is no option but to march to the cadence established by the government or commercialized managed health care systems. Professionalism requires advocacy. Most commonly, this is interpreted as meaning to advocate the clinical interests of the particular client within the context of treatment; indeed, such advocacy is the sine qua non of clinical psychology. Microlevel advocacy, however, should extend to the macrolevel, that is, changing the health care system. Hersch says, "If psychologists mobilize their resources constructively, they can occupy important leadership roles in reshaping the health care system in ways that enhance psychology's opportunities to serve the public's welfare" (p. 25). In the process, they will, of course, be legitimately enhancing their own welfare, namely through improved professional status and employment opportunities.

In conclusion, the future of clinical psychology is bright, but there will be challenges and all psychologists must be prepared to make adaptations. Given the solid nature of the ivory tower, the challenge may be most troublesome for trainers. This is an era when neither trainers nor students can cling to the past. Rather, they must open their minds to new standards and roles. Established practitioners will have to manifest adaptability, thereby becoming equipped to meet requisite accountability and accept new roles and duties. In addition to scientific verification of clinical methods and strategies, the practitioner will need knowledge of law and business. With this professional preparation and personal mind set, employment opportunities will be bountiful. In considering the question posed by Wiggins (1994), "Would you want your child to be a psychologist?" there is ample reason to issue a resounding "Yes, indeed!"

References

Academy of Clinical Psychology (1995), Proliferation of specialties. *Acad. Clin. Psychol. Bull.*, 1(1):unnumbered.

Advance Plan (1990), Psychologists in Medicare in all settings. *Assn. Advance. Psychol./Psychologists for Legislative Action Now*, 1:1 & 3.

Albee, G. (1966–1967), Give us a place to stand and we will move the earth. *Clin. Psychol.*, 20:1–4.

―――― (1970), The uncertain future of clinical psychology. *Amer. Psychol.*, 25:1071–1080.

―――― (1977), The uncertain future of the MA clinical psychologist. *Prof. Psychol.: Res. & Pract.*, 8:122–124.

Alberts, G., & Edelstein, B. A. (1990), Therapist training: A critical review of skill training studies. *Clin. Psychol. Rev.*, 10:497–512.

Allen, G. J., Szollos, S. J., & Williams, B. E. (1986), Doctoral students' comparative evaluations of best and worst psychotherapy supervisors. *Prof. Psychol.: Res. & Pract.*, 17:91–99.

Altman, I. (1987), Centripetal and centrifugal trends in psychology. *Amer. Psychol.*, 42:1058–1069.

American Board of Professional Psychology (ABPP) (1994), Purposes and aims. Unpublished documents. Columbia, MO: ABPP.

―――― (1996), Group psychology is recognized as specialty. *Diplomate*, 15:2, 1, & 3–4.

American Psychiatric Association (1994), *Diagnostic and Statistical Manual of Mental Disorders*, 4th ed. (DSM–IV). Washington, DC: American Psychiatric Press.

American Psychological Association (1975), *Graduate Study in Psychology 1976–77*. Washington, DC: American Psychological Association.

—— Committee on Professional Standards (1981), Specialty guidelines for the delivery of services. *Amer. Psychol.*, 36:639–685.

—— (1983), Door slowly opens for psychologists asking retraining. *APA Monitor*, 14(7):6–7.

—— (1984a), APA-approved sponsors of continuing education in psychology. *Amer. Psychol.*, 39:679–686.

—— Board of Professional Affairs (Sub-committee on Specialization) (1984b), *Specialization in Psychology: Principles*. Washington, DC: American Psychological Association.

—— (1985), APA efforts outlined in report to NIMH advisory council. *APA Monitor*, 16(2):6–7.

—— (1986a), A grand slam helps in '86. *APA Monitor*, 17(2):6–7.

—— (1986b), *Accreditation Handbook*, rev. ed. Washington, DC: Committee on Accreditation and Accreditation Office.

—— (1987a), Model act for state licensure of psychologists. *Amer. Psychol.*, 42:696–703.

—— (1987b), General guidelines for providers of psychological services. *Amer. Psychol.*, 42:712–723.

—— (1988), GOR plan fails: Other avenues of unity sought. *APA Monitor*, 19:1&4.

—— (1989), Final report of the task force on scope and criteria for accreditation. Prepared for the education and training board. Washington, DC: Author.

—— (1990a), Reimbursement under Medicare set for July 1. *APA Monitor*, 21:14.

—— (1990b), Master's graduates suffer identity crisis. *APA Monitor*, 21:28–29.

—— (1992a), Ethical principles of psychologists and code of conduct. *Amer. Psychol.*, 47:1597–1611.

—— (1992b), Rules and procedures. *Amer Psychol.*, 47:1612–1628.

—— (1993a), Guidelines for providers of psychological services to ethnic, linguistic, and culturally diverse populations. *Amer. Psychol.*, 48:45–48.

—— (1993b), *Minority Undergraduate Students of Excellence: 1993 Candidate Listing*. Washington, DC: American Psychological Association.

—— (1993c), APA-accredited predoctoral internships for doctoral training in psychology: 1993. *Amer. Psychol.*, 48:1241–1259.

—— (1993d), APA-accredited doctoral programs in professional psychology: 1993. *Amer. Psychol.*, 48:1260–1270.

—— (1993e), Psychotherapy by telephone. Unpublished document from the Ethics Committee. April 20. Washington, DC: American Psychological Association.

—— (1993f), Psychologists can now screen the elderly. *APA Monitor*, 24:1–21.

—— (1993g), Record keeping guidelines. *Amer. Psychol.*, 48:984–986.

—— (1994a), Guidelines for child custody evaluations in divorce proceedings. *Amer. Psychol.*, 49:677–680.

—— (1994b), Report of the Ethics Committee. *Amer. Psychol.*, 49:659–666.

—— Committee on Accreditation (1994c), *New Accreditation Documents (Including Guidelines and Principles for Accreditation of Programs in Professional Psychology)*. Washington, DC: American Psychological Association.

—— (1994d), APA's council endorses launch of national college. *APA Monitor*, 25:6–7.

—— (1994e), Massachusetts now requires multicultural training. *APA Monitor*, 25:41; 44.

—— (1994f, 1995 addendum), *Graduate Study in Psychology*. Washington, DC: American Psychological Association.

—— (1994g), APA-accredited doctoral programs in professional psychology: 1994. *Amer. Psychol.*, 49:1056–1067.

—— (1994h), APA-accredited predoctoral internships for doctoral trainees in psychology: 1994. *Amer. Psychol.*, 49:1038–1055.

—— (1995), Supplement to listing of APA-accredited doctoral and predoctoral internship training programs in psychology. *Amer. Psychol.*, 50:718–719.

—— Ethics Committee. (1996), Rules and procedures: June 1, 1996. *Amer. Psychol.*, 51(5):529–548.

—— (Undated), *Clinical Psychology*. Brochure available from the Division of Clinical Psychology. Washington, DC: American Psychological Association.

Applebaum, P. S. (1993), Legal liability and managed care. *Amer. Psychol.*, 48:251–257.

Association of Psychology Postdoctoral Internship Centers (APPIC) (1993–1994), *Internship and Postdoctoral Programs in Professional Psychology*, 22nd ed. Washington, DC: APPIC.

Balch, P., & Harper, R. (1976), Prevention, psychologists, and economics: A reply to Wolf. *Prof. Psychol.: Res. & Pract.*, 7:650–653.

Ball, T. J. (1985), Graduate education in psychology: Time for a change? *Amer. Psychol.*, 40:1029–1030.

Barron, J. (1977–1978), An early working draft for special standards in clinical psychology. *Clin. Psychol.*, 31(2):9–17&30.

Baum, B. E., & Gray, J. J. (1992), Expert modeling, self-observation using videotape and acquisition of basic therapy skills. *Prof. Psychol.: Res. & Pract.*, 23:220–225.

Belar, C. D. (1995), Collaboration in capitated care: Challenges for psychology. *Prof. Psychol.: Res. & Pract.*, 26:(2):139–146.

—— Bieliauskas, L. A., Klepac, R. K., Larsen, K. G., Stigall, T. T., & Zimet, C. N. (1993), National conference on postdoctoral training in professional psychology. *Amer. Psychol.*, 48:1284–1289.

—— —— Larsen, K. G., Mensh, I. N., Poey, K., & Roelke, H. J. (1989), National conference on internship training in psychology. *Amer. Psychol.*, 44:60–65.

—— Perry, N. W. (1992), National conference on scientist-practitioner education and training for the professional practice of psychology. *Amer. Psychol.*, 47:71–75.

Bellak, A., & Hersen, M. (1980), *Introduction to Clinical Psychology.* New York: Oxford University Press.

Benton, W. S. (1988), Discovery in professional licensing disciplinary proceedings. *Florida Bar J.*, 62:65–68.

Berman, P. J. (1979), Graduate student selection at the George Washington University. *Clin. Psychol.*, 33(1):10–11.

Bernal, M. E., & Padilla, A. M. (1982), Status of minority curricula and training in clinical psychology. *Amer. Psychol.*, 37:780–787.

Besharov, D. J. (1985), *The Vulnerable Social Worker: Liability for Services Children and Families.* Silver Spring, MD: National Association of Social Workers.

Beutler, L. E., & Fisher, D. (1994), Combined specialty training in counseling, clinical, and school psychology: An idea whose time has returned. *Prof. Psychol.: Res. & Pract.,* 25:62–69.

Bice, T. W. (1981), Social science and health services: Contributions to public policy. In: *Issues in Health Care Policy,* ed. J. B. McKinlay. Cambridge, MA: MIT Press, pp. 1–28.

Binder, J. L. (1993), Is it time to improve psychotherapy training? *Clin. Psychol. Rev.*, 13:301–318.

Bootzin, R. R., & Ruggill, J. S. (1988), Training issues in behavior therapy. *J. Consult. Clin. Psychol.*, 56:703–709.

Broskowski, A. T. (1995), The evolution of health care: Implications for the training and careers of psychologists. *Prof. Psychol.: Res. & Pract.*, 26, 2:156–162.

Caddy, G. (1981), The development and current status of professional psychology. *Prof. Psychol.: Res. & Pract.*, 12:377–384.

CAPP v. Rank, 51 Cul. 3d 1, 793 p. 2d 2 (1990).

Cattell, J. (1937), Retrospect: Psychology as a profession. *J. Consult. Psychol.*, 1:1–3.

Christenson, S. L. (1995). Families and schools: What is the role of the school psychologist? *School Psychol. Quart.*, 10, 2:118–132.

Chronicle of Higher Education (1994), Faculty and staff: Average faculty salaries by rank and field. *Chronicle of Higher Education*, 41:36.

Claiborn, W. L. (1982), The problem of professional incompetence. *Prof. Psychol.: Res. & Pract.*, 13:153–158.

Clement, P. W. (1988), Professional role modeling by faculty: The neglected child in doctoral training. *Prof. Psychol.: Res. & Pract.*, 19:253–254.

Cleveland, S. (1976), Reflections on the rise and fall of psychodiagnosis. *Prof. Psychol.: Res. & Pract.*, 7:309–318.

Clinton, J. J., McCormick, K., & Besteman, J. (1994), Enhancing clinical practice: The role of practice guidelines. *Amer. Psychol.*, 49:30–33.

Committee on Accreditation (1991, Summer), The nature, scope, and implementation of Criterion II: Cultural and individual differences. *Capsule*, pp. 1–5.

Conway, J. B. (1988), Differences among psychologists: Scientists, practitioners, and scientists-practitioners. *Prof. Psychol.: Res. & Pract.*, 19:642–655.

Council for the National Register of Health Service Providers in Psychology (1993), *National Register of Health Service Providers in Psychology*. Washington, DC: Author.

Council of University Directors of Clinical Psychology (February, 1994), Results of Survey of Clinical Directors (N=70): Demographic Composition of Faculty and Graduate Students 1987–1993. San Antonio, TX: Author.

Crane, L. (1925–1926), A plea for the training of psychologists. *J. Abnorm. Soc. Psychol.*, 20:223–228.

Cummings, N. A. (1984), The future of clinical psychology in the United States. *Clin. Psychol.*, 37(1):19–20.

——— (1995), Impact of managed care on employment and training: A primer for survival. *Amer. Psychol.*, 26(1):10–15.

——— VandenBos, G. (1983), Relations with other professions. In: *The Handbook of Clinical Psychology: Theory, Research, and Practice*, Vol. 2, ed. C. E. Walker. Homewood, IL: Dow Jones-Irwin, pp. 1301–1327.

Dale, R. H. I. (1988), State psychological associations, licensing criteria, and the "Master's Issue." *Prof. Psychol.: Res. & Pract.*, 19:589–593.

Dawes, R. M. (1994), *House of Cards: Psychology and Psychotherapy Built on Myth*. New York: Free Press/Macmillan.

DeAngelis, T. (1994), Psychologists' expertise is often essential in court. *APA Monitor*, 25:1,29.

deGroot, G. (1994a), APA seeks to recognize expertise in selected areas. *APA Monitor*, 25:48.

——— (1994b), Clinical psychologists need more science-based training. *APA Monitor*, 25:46.

DeLeon, P. H. (1986), President's message. *Psychother. Bull.*, 21:3–6.

——— (1994), Graduation time—onwards to the future. *Register Report*, 20:16–17.

——— Fox, R. E., & Graham, S. R. (1991), Prescription privileges: Psychology's next frontier? *Amer. Psychol.*, 46:384–393.

——— Frohboese, R., & Meyers, J. (1984), Psychologist on Capitol Hill: A unique use of the skills of the scientist/practitioner. *Prof. Psychol.: Res. & Pract.*, 15:697–705.

——— VandenBos, G., & Kraut, A. (1984), Federal legislation recognizing psychology. *Amer. Psychol.*, 39:933–946.

DeLuca, J. W., & Putnam, S. H. (1993), The professional/technical model in clinical neuropsychology: Deployment characteristics and practical issues. *Prof. Psychol.: Res. & Pract.*, 24:100–106.

DeMuth, N. M., & Kamis, E. (1980), Fees and therapy: Clarification of the relationship of payment source to service utilization. *J. Consult. Clin. Psychol.*, 48:793–795.

Dimond, R., Havens, R., Rathnow, J., & Colliver, J. A. (1977), Employment characteristics of subdoctoral clinical psychologists. *Prof. Psychol.: Res. & Pract.*, 8:116–121.

Dollard, J., & Miller, N. (1950), *Personality and Psychotherapy.* New York: McGraw-Hill.

Dollinger, S. J. (1989), Predictive validity of the Graduate Record Examination in the clinical psychology program. *Prof. Psychol.: Res. & Pract.*, 20:56–58.

Dorken, H. (1977), The practicing psychologist: A growing force in the private sector health care delivery. *Prof. Psychol.: Res. & Pract.*, 8:269–274.

———— (1979), Why the sun didn't set in the west. *Clin. Psychol.*, 33(1):16–17.

———— (1981), Political coping strategies for psychology during a critical decade. *Clin. Psychol.*, 34(3):35.

Dubin, S. (1972), Obsolescence or life-long education: A choice for the professional. *Amer. Psychol.*, 27:486–498.

Eddy, B., Lloyd, P., & Lubin, B. (1987), Enhancing the application to doctoral professional programs: Suggestions from a national survey. *Teach. Psychol.*, 14:160–163.

Edelstein, B. A. (1985), Empirical evaluation of clinical training. *Behav. Therapist*, 8:67–70.

Eggert, M. A., Laughlin, P. R., Hutzell, R. R., Stedman, J. M., Solway, K. S., & Carrington, C. H. (1987), The psychology internship marketplace today. *Prof. Psychol.: Res. & Pract.*, 18:165–171.

Ellis, H. C. (1992), Graduate education in psychology. *Amer. Psychol.*, 47:570–576.

Enright, M. F., Resnick, R. J., DeLeon, P. H., Sciara, A. D., & Tanney, M. F. (1990), The practice of psychology in hospital settings. *Amer. Psychol.*, 45:1059–1065.

———— ———— Ludwigsen, K. R., & DeLeon, P. H. (1993), Hospital practice: Psychology's call to action. *Prof. Psychol.: Res. & Pract.*, 24:135–141.

Erdwins, C. J., & Buffardi, L. C. (1983), Employment of recent M.A.'s in psychology: A middle rung on the career ladder. *Prof. Psychol.: Rev. & Pract.*, 14:112–117.

Etzioni, A., Ed. (1969), *The Semi-Professions and Their Organizations.* New York: Free Press.

Fantuzzo, J. W. (1984), MASTERY: A competency-based training model for clinical psychologists. *Clin. Psychol.*, 37(1):29–30.

Farber, B. A., & Heifetz, L. J. (1981), The satisfactions and stresses of psychotherapeutic work: A factor analytic study. *Prof. Psychol.: Res. & Pract.*, 12:621–630.

Fein, R. (1981), *Social and Economic Attitudes Shaping American Health Policy. Issues in Health Care Policy*, ed. J. B. McKinlay. Cambridge, MA: MIT Press, pp. 29–65.

Fiedler, F. E. (1950), The concept of an ideal therapeutic relationship. *J. Consult. Psychol.*, 14:329–345.

Fisher, K. (1985), Charges catch clinicians in cycle of shame, slipups. *APA Monitor*, 16(5):6–7.

Florida Board of Psychological Examiners (1995), *Laws and Rules*. Tallahassee, FL: Agency for Health Care Administration.

Ford, J. D. (1979), Research on training counselors and clinicians. *Rev. Educat. Res.*, 49:87–130.

Forehand, R. (1985), Training behavioral clinicians for a non-behavioral world. *Behav. Therap.*, 8(1):5–8.

Fowler, R. D. (1990), Psychology: The core discipline. *Amer. Psychol.*, 45:1–6.

———— (1995), Conversation with a concerned member. *APA Monitor*, 26(5):3.

Fox, R. E. (1994), Training professional psychologists for the twenty-first century. *Amer. Psychol.*, 49:200–206.

———— Barclay, A. (1989), Let a thousand flowers bloom: Or, weed the garden? *Amer. Psychol.*, 44:55–59.

———— Kovacs, A. L., & Graham, S. R. (1985), Proposals for a revolution in the preparation and regulation of professional psychologists. *Amer. Psychol.*, 40:1042–1050.

Frank, G. (1984), The Boulder model: History, rationale, and critique. *Prof. Psychol.: Res. & Pract.*, 15:417–435.

Fulero, A. M., & Wilbert, J. R. (1988), Record-keeping practices of clinical and counseling psychologists: A survey of practitioners. *Prof. Psychol.: Res. & Pract.*, 19:658–660.

Gardner, W., & Wilcox, B. L. (1993), Political intervention in scientific peer review. *Amer. Psychol.*, 48:972–983.

Garfield, S. L. (1966), Clinical psychology and the search for identity. *Amer. Psychol.*, 21:353–362.

———— (1982), The emergence of the scientist-practitioner model: Background and rationale. *Clin. Psychol.*, 36(1):4–6.

———— (1992), Comments on "Retrospect: Psychology as a Profession," J. McKeen Catell (1937). *J. Consult. & Clin. Psychol.*, 60:9–15.

———— Kurtz, R. (1976), Clinical psychologists in the 1970s. *Amer. Psychol.*, 31:1–9.

Gehlmann, S. C. (1994), *1993 Employment Survey: Psychology Graduates with Master's, Specialist's, and Related Degrees*. Washington, DC: American Psychological Association.

Gluck, M. R., Babick, A., & Price, K. P. (1979), The use of structured situations in screening applicants to a graduate program in clinical psychology. *Clin. Psychol.*, 33(1):7–8.

Goldenberg, H. (1983), *Contemporary Clinical Psychology*, 2nd ed. Monterey, CA: Brooks/Cole.

Grace, W. C. (1985), Evaluating a prospective clinical internship: Tips for the applicant. *Prof. Psychol.: Res. & Pract.*, 16:475–480.

Graham, S. R. (1989), We are in the hands of Phyllis Stein: A gentle reply to Arthur Kovacs. *Psychother. Bull.*, 24:9–10.

Grilliot, H. J. (1975), *Introduction to Law and the Legal System.* Boston, MA: Houghton Mifflin.

Haas, L. J., & Cummings, N. A. (1991), Managed outpatient mental health plans: Clinical, ethical, and practical guidelines for participation. *Prof. Psychol.: Res. & Pract.*, 22:45–51.

Hadley, J. M. (1961), *Clinical and Counseling Psychology.* New York: Alfred A. Knopf.

Hammond, W. R., & Yung, B. (1993), Minority recruitment and retention practices among schools of professional psychology: A national survey and analysis. *Prof. Psychol.: Res. & Pract.*, 24:3–12.

Harrower, M. R. (1947), *Training in Clinical Psychology.* New York: Josiah Macey, Jr. Foundation.

Havens, R. A. (1979), A brief review of the current MA controversy. *Prof. Psychol.: Res. & Pract.*, 10:185–188.

―――― Colliver, J. A., Dimond, R. E., & Wesley, R. M. (1982), Ph.D. and MA clinical psychologists and MSWs in public mental health settings: A nationwide comparison. *Prof. Psychol.: Res. & Pract.*, 13:654–660.

Hersch, L. (1995), Adapting to health care reform and managed care: Three strategies for survival and growth. *Prof. Psychol.: Res. & Pract.*, 26(1):16–26.

Hess, A. K., & Hess, K. A. (1983), Psychotherapy supervision: A survey of internship training practices. *Prof. Psychol.: Res. & Pract.*, 14:504–513.

Highlen, P. S. (1994), Racial/ethnic diversity in doctoral programs of psychology: Challenges for the twenty-first century. *Appl. & Prevent. Psychology*, 3:91–108.

Hills, H. I., & Strozier, A. L. (1992), Multicultural training in APA-approved counseling psychology programs: A survey. *Prof. Psychol.: Res. & Pract.*, 23:43–51.

Hirschberg, N., & Itkin, S. (1978), Graduate student success in psychology. *Amer. Psychol.*, 33:1083–1093.

Hobbs, N. (1964), Mental health's third revolution. *Amer. J. Orthopsychiat.*, 34:822–833.

Hogan, D. B. (1979), *The Regulation of Psychotherapists, Vol. III. A Review of Malpractice Suits in the United States.* Cambridge, MA: Ballinger.

Hosticka, C., Hibbard, M., & Sundberg, N. (1983), Improving psychologists' contribution to the policy making process. *Prof. Psychol.: Res. & Pract.*, 14:374–385.

Hotaling, D. (1994), New Ph.D.'s can find a life outside academe. *Chron. Higher Ed.*, 41:B-1–2.

Inouye, D. K. (1984), VA diplomates to receive bonus. *Diplomate*, 4:2, 1.

Jacobson, N. (1995), The overselling of therapy. *Fam. Ther. Networker*, 19(2):41–47.

Jastrow, J. (1930), Autobiography. In: *A History of Psychology in Autobiography*, Vol. 1, ed. C. Murchison. Worcester, MA: Clark University Press.

Johnson, W. B., & Wilson, K. (1993), The military internship: A retrospective analysis. *Prof. Psychol.: Res. & Pract.*, 24:312–318.

Joint Commission on Mental Illness and Health (1961), *Action for Mental Health*. New York: Basic Books.

Jones, R. T. (1989), A salute to the founding mothers and fathers of clinical psychology. *Clin. Psychol.*, 42:19–28.

Julius, S., & Handal, P. (1980), Third-party payment and national health insurance: An update of psychology's efforts toward inclusion. *Prof. Psychol.: Res. & Pract.*, 11:955–964.

Kalafat, J., & Neigher, W. (1983), Can quality survive in public mental health programs? The challenges for training. *Prof. Psychol.: Res. & Pract.*, 14:90–104.

Kalinkowitz, B. (1978), Scientist-practitioner—The widening schism. *Clin. Psychol.*, 32(1):4–7.

Karon, B. P. (1995a), Becoming a first-rate professional psychologist despite graduate education. *Prof. Psychol.: Res. & Pract.*, 26(2):211–217.

———— (1995b), Provision of psychotherapy under managed health care: A growing crisis and national nightmare. *Prof. Psychol.: Res. & Pract.*, 26(1):5–19.

Kaslow, N. J., & Rice, D. G. (1985), Developmental stresses of psychology internship training: What training staff can do to help. *Prof. Psychol.: Res. & Pract.*, 16:253–261.

Katkin, E. (1982), On reliable knowledge and the proliferation of professional schools of psychology. *Clin. Psychol.*, 36(1):9–11.

Kelly, E. (1961), Clinical psychology—1960 report of survey findings. *Newsl.: Div. Clin. Psychol.*, 14:1–11.

Kempler, H., & Norman, M. (1981), Difficulties of a psychologist's participation in legislative matters. *Clin. Psychol.*, 34(3):30–31.

Kerlinger, F. N. (1964), *Foundation of Behavioral Research*. New York: Holt, Rinehart & Winston.

Kirsch, I., & Winter, C. (1983), A history of clinical psychology. In: *The Handbook of Clinical Psychology*, Vol. 1, ed. C. E. Walker. Homewood, IL: Dow Jones-Irwin.

Knapp, S. J., & VandeCreek, L. (1985), Psychotherapy and privileged communications in child custody cases. *Prof. Psychol.: Res. & Pract.*, 16:398–407.

Kohout, J., & Wicherski, M. (1991), *1989 Doctorate Employment Survey*. Washington, DC: American Psychological Association.

Kolbe, K., Shemberg, K., & Leventhal, D. (1985), University training in psychodiagnostics and psychotherapy. *Clin. Psychol.*, 38(3): 593–661.

Korchin, S. (1976), *Modern Clinical Psychology*. New York: Basic Books.

Korman, M. (1974), National conference on levels and patterns of professional training in psychology. *Amer. Psychol.*, 29:441–449.

Krause, A. A., & Lawlor, R. (1990), Internship selection and early acceptance procedure: Students' evaluation. *Prof. Psychol.: Res. & Pract.*, 21:144–146.

Lamb, D. H., Cochran, D. J., & Jackson, V. R. (1991), Training and organizational issues associated with identifying and responding to intern impairment. *Prof. Psychol.: Res. & Pract.*, 22:291–296.

Lawler, E. E., III (1981), *Pay and Organization Development*. Reading, MA: Addison-Wesley.

Levy, C. (1981), Improving patient care. Psychologist parity with psychiatrists in hospitals. *Clin. Psychol.*, 34(3):24–25.

Levy, L. H. (1983), Evaluation of students in clinical psychology programs: A program evaluation perspective. *Prof. Psychol.: Res. & Pract.*, 12:497–503.

———— (1984), The metamorphosis of clinical psychology: Toward a new chapter as a human services psychology. *Amer. Psychol.*, 39:486–494.

Litwin, W. S., Boswell, D. L., & Kraft, W. A. (1991), Medical staff membership and clinical privileges: A survey of hospital affiliated psychologists. *Prof. Psychol.: Res. & Pract.*, 22:322–327.

Louttit, C. M. (1939), The nature of clinical psychology. *Psychol. Bull.*, 36:361–389.

Ludwigsen, K. R., & Albright, D. G. (1994), Training psychologists for hospital practice: A proposal. *Prof. Psychol.: Res. & Pract.*, 25:241–246.

Machover, K. (1980), Reflections of a pioneer: A personal diary of over fifty years in clinical psychology. *Clin. Psychol.*, 34:5–7.

Magaro, P. A., Gripp, R., & McDowell, D. J. (1978), *The Mental Health Industry*. New York: John Wiley.

Matarazzo, J. (1980), Behavioral health and behavioral medicine. *Amer. Psychol.*, 35:807–817.

Matarazzo, J. D. (1987), There is only one psychology, no specialties, but many applications. *Amer. Psychol.*, 42:893–903.

———— (1992), Psychological testing and assessment in the 21st century. *Amer. Psychol.*, 47:1007–1018.

Matulef, N. J., Pottharst, K. E., & Rothenberg, P. J., Eds. (1970), *The Revolution in Professional Training*. Washington, DC: National Council on Graduate Education in Psychology.

Mayne, T. J., Norcross, J. C., & Sayette, M. A. (1994), Admission requirements, acceptance rates, and financial assistance in clinical psychology programs. *Amer. Psychol.*, 49:806–811.

McConnell, S. (1984), Doctor of psychology degree: From hibernation to reality. *Prof. Psychol.: Res. & Pract.*, 15:362–370.

McFall, R. M. (1995), The future of mental-health care. *Chron. Higher Ed.*, 41(45):B-1–3.

McGuire, J. M., Toal, P., & Blau, B. (1985), The adult client's conception of confidentiality in the therapeutic relationship. *Prof. Psychol.: Res. & Pract.*, 16:375–384.

Meade, V. (1994), Psychologists forecast future of the profession. *APA Monitor*, 25:14.

Meltzoff, J. (1984), Research training for clinical psychologists. *Prof. Psychol.: Res. & Pract.*, 15:203–209.

Merrikin, K. J., Overcast, T. D., & Sales, B. D. (1987), Recognition of psychologists in workers' compensation law. *Prof. Psychol.: Res. & Pract.*, 18:260–264.

Meyer, R. G. (1980), Legal and procedural issues in the evaluation of clinical graduate students. *Clin. Psychol.*, 33(4):15–17.

Miller, H. L., & Rickard, H. C. (1983), Procedures and students' rights in the evaluation process. *Prof. Psychol.: Res. & Pract.*, 14:830–836.

Mio, J. S., & Morris, D. R. (1990), Cross-cultural issues in psychology training programs. *Prof. Psychol.: Res. & Pract.*, 21:434–441.

Moskowitz, S. A., & Rupert, P. A. (1983), Conflict resolution within the supervisory relationship. *Prof. Psychol.: Res. & Pract.*, 14:632–641.

Mowbray, C., Miller, B., & Schneider, L. (1983), The new federalism and state mental health agencies: Roles for psychologists. *Prof. Psychol.: Res. & Pract.*, 14:386–399.

Mozdzierz, G. J., Snodgrass, R. W., & DeLeon, P. H. (1992), A new role for psychologist–hospital ethics committees. *Prof. Psychol.: Res. & Pract.*, 23:493–499.

Muehleman, T., Pickens, B. K., & Robinson, F. (1985), Informing clients about the limits of confidentiality, risks, and their rights: Is self-disclosure inhibited? *Prof. Psychol.: Res. & Pract.*, 16:385–397.

Munoz, R. F., Hollon, S. D., McGrath, E., Rehm, L. P., & VandenBos, G. R. (1994), On the AHCPR depression in primary care guidelines. *Amer. Psychol.*, 49, 1:42– 61.

Murray, B. (1995), School-based clinics get a boost from CDC. *APA Monitor*, 26(7):56.

National Science Foundation (1988), *Profiles—Psychology; Human Resource and Funding.* NSF Special Report 88-325. Washington, DC: U.S. Government Printing Office.

Newman, A. S. (1981), Ethical issues in the supervision of psychotherapy. *Prof. Psychol.: Res. & Pract.*, 9:690–695.

Newman, R., & Bricklin, P. M. (1991), Parameters of managed health care: Legal, ethical, and professional guidelines. *Prof. Psychol.: Res. & Pract.*, 22:26–35.

Nietzel, M. T., Bernstein, D. A., & Milich, R. (1994), *Introduction to Clinical Psychology*, 4th ed. Englewood Cliffs, NJ: Prentice-Hall.

Norcross, J. C., & Prochaska, J. O. (1982a), A national survey of clinical psychologists: Affiliations and orientations. *Clin. Psychol.*, 35(3):4–6.

—— —— (1982b), A national survey of clinical psychologists: Characteristics and activities. *Clin. Psychol.*, 35(2):5–8.

—— —— (1982c), A national survey of clinical psychologists: Views on training, career choice, and APA. *Clin. Psychol.*, 35(4):1&3–6.

—— —— Gallagher, K. M. (1989a), Clinical psychologists in the 1980s: I. Demographics, affiliations, and satisfactions. *Clin. Psychol.*, 42:29–39.

—— —— (1989b), Clinical psychologists in the 1980s: II. Theory, research, and practice. *Clin. Psychol.*, 42:45–53.

—— Stevenson, J. F. (1984), How shall we judge ourselves? Training evaluations in clinical psychology. *Prof. Psychol.: Res. & Pract.*, 15:497–508.

—— —— Nash, J. M. (1986), Evaluation of internship training: Practices, problems, and prospects. *Prof. Psychol.: Res. & Pract.*, 17:280–282.

Novack, T. A. (1987), Update on social security disability determination for the mentally impaired. *Prof. Psychol.: Res. & Pract.*, 18:265–268.

Nyman, L. (1973), Some odds on getting into Ph.D. programs in clinical psychology and counseling psychology. *Amer. Psychol.*, 36:934–935.

O'Donohue, W., Plaud, J. J., Mowatt, A. M., & Fearon, J. R. (1989), Current status of curricula of doctoral training programs in clinical psychology. *Prof. Psychol.: Res. & Pract.*, 20:196–197.

Olson, S. K., Downing, N. E., Heppner, P. P., & Pinkey, J. (1986), Is there life after graduate school? Coping with the transition to postdoctoral employment. *Prof. Psychol.: Res. & Pract.*, 17:415–419.

O'Sullivan, J. J., & Quevillon, R. P. (1992), 40 years later: Is the Boulder model still alive? *Amer. Psychol.*, 4:67–70.

Parker, L. E., & Detterman, D. K. (1988), The balance between clinical and research interests among Boulder model graduate students. *Prof. Psychol.: Res. & Pract.*, 19:342–344.

Perlman, B. (1985), A national survey of APA-affiliated master-level clinicians: Description and comparison. *Prof. Psychol.*, 16:553–564.

Peterson, D., & Stricker, G., Eds. (1986), *Quality Assurance in Professional School Education.* Washington, DC: American Psychological Association.

Peterson, D. R. (1968), The doctor of psychology program at the University of Illinois. *Amer. Psychol.*, 4:511–516.

—— (1976), Is psychology a profession? *Amer. Psychol.*, 31:572–581.

—— (1985), Twenty years of practitioner training in psychology. *Amer. Psychol.*, 40:441–451.

—— (1991), Connection and disconnection of research and practice in the education of professional psychologists. *Amer. Psychol.*, 46:422–429.

Petzel, T. P., & Berndt, D. J. (1980), APA internship selection criteria: Relative importance of academic and clinical preparation. *Prof. Psychol.: Res. & Pract.,* 11:792–796.

Phares, E. J. (1992), *Clinical Psychology: Concepts, Methods, & Profession,* 4th ed. Pacific Grove, CA: Brooks/Cole.

Phillips, B. N. (1989), Role of the practitioner in applying science to practice. *Prof. Psychol.: Res. & Pract.,* 20:3–8.

Pion, G. M. (1991), A national human resource agenda for psychology: The need for a broader perspective. *Prof. Psychol.: Res. & Pract.,* 22:449–455.

Piotrowski, C., & Keller, J. W. (1984), Psychodiagnostic testing in APA-approved clinical psychology programs. *Prof. Psychol.: Res. & Pract.,* 15:450–456.

——— Zalewski, C. (1993), Training in psychodiagnostic testing in APA-approved PsyD and PhD clinical psychology programs. *J. Personal. Assess.,* 61:394–405.

Poffenberger, A. T. (1938), The training of a clinical psychologist. *J. Consult. Psychol.,* 2:1–6.

Putnam, S. H., & Anderson, C. (1994), The second TCN salary survey: A survey of neuropsychologists part I. *Clin. Neuropsychol.,* 8:3–37.

Raimy, V. (1950), *Training in Clinical Psychology.* New York: Prentice-Hall.

Range, L. M., Menyhert, A., Walsh, M. L., Hardin, K. N., Ellis, J. B., & Craddick, R. (1991), Letters of recommendation: Perspective, recommendations, and ethics. *Prof. Psychol.: Res. & Pract.,* 22:389–392.

Reeves, T. Z., & Torrez, M. L. (1994), *Managing Human Resources.* St. Paul, MN: West.

Reisman, J. (1981), History and current trends in clinical psychology. In: *Clinical Practice of Psychology,* ed. C. E. Walker. New York: Pergamon Press.

——— (1991), *A History of Clinical Psychology,* 2nd. ed. New York: Hemisphere Publishing Corporation.

Resnick, R. (1983), Medicaid: Direct provider recognition. *Prof. Psychol.: Res. & Pract.,* 14:368–373.

Rickard, H. C., & Bernaty, M. L. (1983), Delimiting subspecialty clinical training. *Clin. Psychol.,* 36(3):75–78.

——— Clements, C. B. (1986), An evaluation of interviewed versus noninterviewed clinical psychology students. *Prof. Psychol.: Res. & Pract.,* 17:78–79.

——— ——— (1993), Critique of APA accreditation criterion II: Cultural and individual differences. *Prof. Psychol.: Res. & Pract.,* 24:123–126.

Robiner, W. N. (1991), How many psychologists are needed? A call for a national psychology human resource agenda. *Prof. Psychol.: Res. & Pract.,* 22:427–440, 461–463.

Robyak, J., & Goodyear, R. (1984), Graduate school origins of diplomates and fellows in professional psychology. *Prof. Psychol.: Res. & Pract.,* 15:379–387.

Rogers, C. R. (1942), *Counseling and Psychotherapy.* Boston: Houghton Mifflin.

—— (1951), *Client-centered Therapy.* Boston: Houghton Mifflin.

Ross, M. J., Holzman, L. A., Handal, P. J., & Gilner, F. H. (1991), Performance on the examination for the professional practice of psychology as a function of specialty, degree, administrative housing, and accreditation status. *Prof. Psychol.: Res. & Pract.*, 22:347–350.

Ross, R. R., & Altmaier, E. M. (1989), Implications of personnel psychology for intern selection. *Prof. Psychol.: Res. & Pract.*, 20:221–228.

Russell, R. K., & Petrie, T. (1994), Issues in training effective supervisors. *Appl. & Prevent. Psychol.*, 3:27–42.

Sanchez-Hucles, J., & Cash, T. F. (1992), The dissertation in professional psychology programs: I. A survey of clinical directors on requirements and practices. *Prof. Psychol.: Res. & Pract.*, 23:59–62.

Sayette, M. A., & Mayne, T. J. (1990), Survey of current clinical and research trends in clinical psychology. *Amer. Psychol.*, 45: 1263–1266.

Schacht, T. E. (1984), Toward a rational clinical training system. *Clin. Psychol.*, 37(1):26–27.

Schaefer, A. B. (1981), Clinical supervision. In: *Clinical Practice of Psychology*, ed. C. E. Walker. New York: Pergamon, pp. 50–61.

Schein, E. H. (1978), *Career Dynamics: Matching Individual Organizational Needs.* Reading, MA: Addison-Wesley.

Schneider, A. (1980), Psychologists in comprehensive health care settings. *Clin. Psychol.*, 33(4):8–9.

Schneider, S. F. (1981), Where have all the students gone? Positions of psychologists trained in clinical/service programs. *Amer. Psychol.*, 36:1427–1449.

—— (1991), No fluoride in our future. *Prof. Psychol.: Res. & Pract.*, 22:456–460.

Schofield, W. (1969), The role of psychologists in the delivery of health services. *Amer. Psychol.*, 24:565–584.

Schulberg, H. C., & Rush, A. J. (1994), Clinical practice guidelines for managing major depression in primary care practice: Implications for psychologists. *Amer. Psychol.*, 49(1):34–41.

Schulman, M. E. (1988), Cost containment in clinical psychology: Critique of Biodyne and the HMOs. *Prof. Psychol.*, 19:298–307.

Sechrest, L. (1992), The past future of clinical psychology: A reflection on Woodworth (1937). *J. Consult. Clin. Psychol.*, 60:18–23.

Sechrest, L. B. (1985), Specialization? Who needs it? *Clin. Psychol.*, 38:1–3.

Shakow, D., Hilgard, E. R., Kelly, E. L., Luckey, B., Sanford, R. N., & Shaffer, L. F. (1947), Recommended graduate training program in clinical psychology. *Amer. Psychol.*, 2:539–558.

Shapiro, A. F., & Wiggins, J. G. (1994), A PsyD degree for every practitioner. *Amer. Psychol.*, 49:207–210.

Shemberg, K., Keeley, S. M., & Blum, M. (1989), Attitudes toward traditional and nontraditional dissertation research: Survey of directors of clinical training. *Prof. Psychol.: Res. & Pract.*, 20:190–192.

Shemberg, K. M., & Leventhal, D. B. (1981), Attitudes of internships directors toward preinternship training and clinical training models. *Prof. Psychol.: Res. & Pract.*, 12:639–646.

Simon, G. (1975), Psychology and the "Treatment Rights Movement." *Prof. Psychol.: Res. & Pract.*, 6(3):243–251.

Sleek, S. (1995a), Group therapy: Tapping the power of teamwork. *APA Monitor*, 26(7):1 & 38–39.

———— (1995b), Psychologists take on new roles on health-care team. *APA Monitor*, 26(6):25.

Smith, M. B. (1990), Psychology in the public interest: What have we done? What can we do? *Amer. Psychol.*, 45:530–536.

Smyer, M. A., Balster, R. L., Egli, D., Johnson, D. L., Kilbey, M. M., Leith, N. J., & Puente, A. E. (1993), Summary of the report of the ad hoc task force on psychopharmacology of the American Psychological Association. *Prof. Psychol.: Res. & Pract.*, 24:394–403.

Snepp, F. P., & Peterson, D. R. (1988), Evaluative comparison of PsyD and PhD students by clinical internship supervisors. *Prof. Psychol.: Res. & Pract.*, 19:180–183.

Solway, K. S., Huntley, D. K., Stedman, J. M., Laughlin, P. R., Belar, C. D., Flynn, M. F., & Carrington, C. H. (1987), Survey of non-APA-accredited internships and their interns. *Prof. Psychol.: Res. & Pract.*, 18:176–178.

Stampelos, C. A., & Jones, D. P. (1990), What your client should do when the Department of Professional Regulation investigates him. *Florida Bar J.*, 64:68–70.

Stapp, J., Fulcher, R., & Wicherski, M. (1984), The employment of 1981 and 1982 doctorate recipients in psychology. *Amer. Psychol.*, 39:1408–1423.

———— Tucker, A. M., & VandenBos, G. R. (1985), Census of psychological personnel: 1983. *Amer. Psychol.*, 40:1317–1351.

Starr, P. (1994), *The Logic of Health Care Reform: Why and How the President's Plan Will Work*, rev. ed. New York: Penguin (Whittle).

Stedman, J. M. (1989, Spring), The intern marketplace: Issues of supply and demand. *Assn. Psychol. Internship Centers Newsletter*, 45–49.

Steinhauser, L. (1985), A new Ph.D.'s search for work: A case study. *J. Counsel. Develop.*, 63:300–303.

Steinpreis, R., Queen, L., & Tennen, H. (1992), The education of clinical psychologists: A survey of training directors. *Clin. Psychol.*, 45:87–100.

Sterling, M. (1982), Must psychology lose its soul? *Prof. Psychol.: Res. & Pract.*, 36:789–796.

Stevens, J., Yock, T., & Perlman, B. (1979), Comparing master's clinical training with professional responsibilities in community mental health centers. *Prof. Psychol.: Res. & Pract.*, 10:20–27.

Stevenson, J. F., & Norcross, J. C. (1985), Evaluation activity in psychology training clinics: National survey findings. *Prof. Psychol.: Res. & Pract.*, 16:29–41.

Stigall, T. (1981), Sunset on licensure: Are professional ethics enough? *Clin. Psychol.*, 34(3):28–29.

Stricker, G. (1983), Respecialization in clinical psychology: The Adelphi model. *Clin. Psychol.*, 36(3):62–63.

—— (1984), Clinical training and accountability in service delivery. *Clin. Psychol.*, 37(1):27–28.

—— (1992), The relationship of research to practice. *Amer. Psychol.*, 47:543–549.

—— Cohen, L. (1984), APA/Campus peer review project: Implications for research and practice. *Prof. Psychol.: Res. & Pract.*, 15:96–108.

—— Hull, J. W., & Woodring, J. (1984), Respecialization in clinical psychology. *Prof. Psychol.: Res. & Pract.*, 15:210–217.

Strickland, B. R. (1983a), Responding to current concerns in clinical psychology. *Clin. Psychol.*, 36(2):25, 27.

—— (1983b), Chance and choice. *Clin. Psychol.*, 36(4):82,85.

—— (1985), Over the boulders and through the vail. *Clin. Psychol.*, 38(3):52–56.

Strupp, H. H. (1955), Psychotherapeutic technique, professional affiliation, and experience level. *J. Consult. Psychol.*, 19:97–102.

—— (1982), Some observations on clinical psychology. *Clin. Psychol.*, 36:6–7.

Sturgis, D. K., Verstegen, J. P., Randolph, D. L., & Garvin, R. B. (1980), Professional psychology internships. *Prof. Psychol.*, 11:567–573.

Sue, D. A. (1991), A model for cultural diversity training. *J. Counsel. & Devel.*, 70:99–105.

Super, D. E. (1955), Transition: From vocational guidance to counseling psychology. *J. Counsel. Psychol.*, 2:3–9.

Syverson, P. D. (1982), Two decades of doctorates in psychology: A comparison with national trends. *Amer. Psychol.*, 37:1203–1212.

Talley, J. E. (1990), Salary survey of ABPP counseling psychology diplomates. *Counsel. Psychol.*, 18:504.

Tipton, R. M. (1983), Clinical and counseling psychology: A study of roles and functions. *Prof. Psychol.: Res. & Pract.*, 14:837–846.

—— Watkins, C. E., & Ritz, S. (1991), Selection, training, and career preparation of predoctoral interns in psychology. *Prof. Psychol.: Res. & Pract.*, 22:60–67.

Tryon, G. S., & Tryon, W. W. (1986), Factors associated with clinical practicum trainee's engagement of clients in counseling. *Prof. Psychol.: Res. & Pract.*, 17:586–589.

Tucker, G. H., & Annis, L. V. (1981), The ideal function of the terminal master's degree program for a Ph.D.-pursuing student. *Prof. Psychol.: Res. & Pract.*, 12:336–340.

Tyler, J. D., & Clark, J. A. (1987), Clinical psychologists reflect on the usefulness of various components of graduate training, *Prof. Psychol.: Res. & Pract.*, 18:381–384.

VandeCreek, L., & Knapp, S. (1993), *Tarasoff and Beyond: Legal and Clinical Considerations in the Treatment of Life-Endangering Patients*, rev. ed. Sarasota, FL: Professional Resource Press.

———— ———— Brace, K. (1990), Mandatory CE for licensed psychologists: Its rationale and implementation. *Prof. Psychol.: Res. & Pract.*, 21:135–140.

VandenBos, G. R., DeLeon, P. H., & Belar, C. D. (1991), How many psychological practitioners are needed? It's too early to know! *Prof. Psychol.: Res. & Pract.*, 22:441–448.

———— Stapp, J. (1983), Service providers in psychology: Results of the 1982 APA human resources survey. *Amer. Psychol.*, 38:1330–1352.

Vane, J. R. (1985), School psychology: To be or not to be. *J. School Psychol.*, 23:101–112.

Walfish, S., & Coovert, D. L. (1989), Beginning and maintaining an independent practice. *Prof. Psychol.: Res. & Pract.*, 20:54–55.

———— Polifka, J. A., & Stenmark, D. E. (1985), Career satisfaction in clinical psychology: A survey of recent graduates. *Prof. Psychol.: Res. & Pract.*, 16:576–580.

———— Stenmark, D. E., Shealy, J. S., & Shealy, S. E. (1989), Reasons why applicants select clinical psychology graduate programs. *Prof. Psychol.: Res. & Pract.*, 20:350–354.

———— Sumprer, G. F. (1984), Employment opportunities for graduates of APA-approved and nonapproved training programs. *Amer. Psychol.*, 39:1199–1200.

Weiss, L., & Weiss, B. W. (1992), Personal reminiscences of a psychologist married couple on changing perspectives in 20 years of professional psychology. *Prof. Psychol.: Res. & Pract.*, 23:349–352.

Weitz, R. D. (1992), A half century of psychological practice. *Prof. Psychol.: Res. & Pract.*, 23:448–452.

Wicherski, M., & Kohout, J. (1995), *1994–95 Faculty Salaries in Graduate Programs of Psychology*. Washington, DC: American Psychological Association.

———— ———— (1996), *1995–96 Faculty Salaries in Graduate Departments of Psychology*. Washington, DC: American Psychological Association.

Wiens, A. N. (1993), Postdoctoral education-training for specialty practice: Long anticipated, finally realized. *Amer. Psychol.*, 48:415–422.

Wierzbicki, M. (1993), *Issues in Clinical Psychology: Subjective Versus Objective Approaches*. Boston: Allyn & Bacon.

Wiggins, J. G. (1984), New-JCAH policy: psychologists' victory. *Clin. Psychol.*, 43:51–52.

———— (1990), Re-defining clinical psychology in the changing health care market. *Clin. Psychol.*, 43:51–52.

———— (1994), Would you want your child to be a psychologist? *Amer. Psychol.*, 49:485–492.

Wolfe, D. (1946), The reorganized APA. *Amer. Psychol.*, 1:3–6.

Woody, R. H. (1983a), Avoiding malpractice in psychotherapy. In: *Innovations in Clinical Practice: A Source Book*, Vol. 2, ed. P. A. Keller & L. G. Ritt. Sarasota, FL: Professional Resource Exchange, pp. 205–216.

———— (1983b), Techniques in handling psychological cases. In: *Handbook of Clinical Psychology: Theory, Research, and Practice*, Vol. 2, ed. C. E. Alker. Homewood, IL: Dow Jones-Irwin, pp. 1420–1439.

———— (1984), Professional responsibilities and liabilities. In: *The Law and the Practice of Human Services*, ed. R. H. Woody. San Francisco, CA: Jossey-Bass, pp. 272–401.

———— (1985), Public policy, malpractice law, and the mental health professional: Some legal and clinical guidelines. In: *Psychology, Psychiatry, and the Law*, ed. C. P. Ewing. Sarasota, FL: Professional Resource Exchange, pp. 509–525.

———— (1988a), *Fifty Ways to Avoid Malpractice: A Guidebook for Mental Health Professionals*. Sarasota, FL: Professional Resource Exchange.

———— (1988b), *Protecting Your Mental Health Practice: How to Minimize Legal and Financial Risk*. San Francisco: Jossey-Bass.

———— (1991), *Quality Care in Mental Health: Assuring the Best Clinical Services*. San Francisco: Jossey-Bass.

———— (1994a), Being realistic about legal complaints. *FL Psychologist*, 44:19–20.

———— (1994b), The essential psychological record in 1994. *FL Psychologist*, 44:13–14.

———— LaVoie, J. C., & Epps, S. (1992), *School Psychology: A Developmental and Social Systems Approach*. Boston: Allyn & Bacon.

———— Robertson, M. H. (1988), *Becoming a Clinical Psychologist*. Madison, CT: International Universities Press.

Wright, L. (1983), Please don't tell my mother I'm a clinical psychologist—She still thinks I play piano in a brothel. *Clin. Psychol.*, 36(2):49–51.

Wright, R. H. (1981a), Psychologists and professional liability (malpractice) insurance: A retrospective review. *Amer. Psychol.*, 36:1485–1493.

———— (1981b), What to do until the malpractice lawyer comes: A survivor's manual. *Amer Psychol.*, 36:1535–1541.

———— (1992), The American Psychological Association and the rise of advocacy. *Prof. Psychol.*, 23:443–447.

Wyckoff, D. M. (1990), Evidentiary standards in formal administrative proceedings. *FL Bar J.*, 64:67–69.

Zaro, J., Batchelor, W., Ginsberg, M., & Pallak, M. (1982), Psychology and the JCAH: Reflections on a decade of struggle. *Amer. Psychol.*, 37:1342–1349.

Name Index

Subject Index